The Complete
UK Air Fryer Cookbook
2023

1900-Day Yummy, Juicy and Healthy Recipes For Beginners
to Master the Art of Air Frying Using British ingredients

Allison C. Olson

Contents

Introduction

Welcome to the delightful world of culinary exploration! In this recipe book, we invite you to embark on a journey filled with mouthwatering dishes, vibrant flavors, and healthy choices. Whether you're an experienced home cook or a novice in the kitchen, this collection of recipes has something for everyone.

In the world of cooking, traditions hold a special place in our hearts. They remind us of cherished family gatherings, passed-down recipes, and the comforting flavours of home. With the air fryer, you have the power to take those beloved traditional recipes and give them a modern twist while keeping them healthier.

In this recipe book, you will find a collection of traditional family favourites that have been thoughtfully adapted to suit the air fryer's cooking method. We understand the importance of preserving the essence of these classic dishes while embracing a healthier approach to cooking. By replacing deep frying with air frying, we have transformed these dishes into lighter, yet equally delicious versions of themselves.

Imagine enjoying crispy chicken nuggets, perfectly golden fish and chips, or flavourful potato skins, all cooked to perfection in the air fryer. These recipes not only capture the essence of our family traditions but also showcase the versatility of the air fryer in recreating beloved flavours and textures. The air fryer's hot circulating air ensures that your dishes come out with a satisfying crunch on the outside, while keeping the inside tender and juicy.

We understand that adapting traditional recipes can be a delicate process, requiring attention to detail and a deep understanding of flavours and techniques. That's why each recipe in this collection has been carefully tested and perfected to ensure exceptional results. We have taken the time to consider the nuances of each dish, making adjustments to cooking times, temperatures, and ingredient proportions to achieve the best outcome in the air fryer.

By incorporating these adapted recipes into your cooking repertoire, you can continue to enjoy the comforting familiarity of your family's favourite dishes while embracing a healthier cooking method. The air fryer allows you to achieve that delightful crispy texture without the need for excessive oil, making your meals lighter and more nutritious.

We hope that by sharing these adaptations, we inspire you to revisit your own treasured recipes and reimagine them with the magic of the air fryer. It's an opportunity to honour the past while embracing a healthier future, and we're excited to guide you through this culinary journey of adapting traditional recipes for the air fryer.

So, gather your loved ones, gather your traditional recipes, and get ready to embark on a flavourful adventure. Let the air fryer be your trusty companion as you recreate the dishes that hold a special place in your heart, infused with the health-conscious benefits of modern cooking techniques. Together, let's celebrate the traditions that have shaped us while embracing the joy of healthier eating.

As you embark on this culinary adventure, we encourage you to approach each recipe with a spirit of curiosity and creativity. Feel free to adapt and modify the recipes to suit your taste preferences and dietary needs. Experiment with different ingredients, herbs, and spices to make each dish uniquely yours.

Whether you're seeking healthy vegetable-centric meals, quick and easy family favourites, or flavourful staples and sauces, this recipe book has been crafted to inspire and guide you on your culinary journey. With each recipe, we aim to ignite your passion for cooking, nourish your body and soul, and create memorable moments around the dining table.

So, tie on your apron, preheat your air fryer, and let the aroma of delicious creations fill your kitchen. It's time to embark on a culinary adventure that will tantalise your taste buds, nourish your body, and bring joy to your everyday cooking. Get ready to indulge in a world of flavours and embrace the joy of homemade meals that will leave you longing for more.

But why choose an air fryer as your cooking companion?

Here are 10 reasons to use an air fryer:

Healthier Cooking: Air fryers use significantly less oil than traditional deep frying, reducing the fat content in your dishes while still delivering crispy and delicious results.

Versatility: Air fryers can do more than just fry. They can also grill, roast, bake, and even reheat leftovers, giving you a wide range of cooking options in one appliance.

Time-Saving: Air fryers cook food faster than conventional ovens, saving you precious time in the kitchen. You can enjoy your favourite dishes in less time without compromising on taste and texture.

Energy Efficiency: Air fryers are more energy-efficient than traditional ovens, making them a greener choice for environmentally conscious individuals.

Easy Cleanup: With their non-stick cooking surfaces and removable parts, air fryers are a breeze to clean up. Simply wipe them down or put the parts in the dishwasher for effortless maintenance.

Crispy Texture: Air fryers produce a satisfyingly crispy exterior on foods without the need for excessive oil.

Enjoy guilt-free indulgence with that desirable crunch.

Even Cooking: The circulating hot air in an air fryer ensures that food is cooked evenly on all sides, eliminating

Healthier Ingredients: By using an air fryer, you can enjoy healthier versions of your favourite dishes by reducing the need for added fats and oils. You can still achieve a golden and crispy texture without sacrificing flavour or nutrition.

Compact and Space-Saving: Air fryers are typically compact appliances that take up minimal counter space. They are perfect for smaller kitchens or those who prefer to keep their countertops organised and clutter-free.

Reduced Odor and Smoke: Air fryers help minimize the lingering smells and smoke often associated with traditional frying methods. Enjoy cooking without filling your kitchen with unwanted odors, and experience a more pleasant cooking environment.

How do Airfryers differ from Deep Fat Fryers?

Air fryers and deep-fat fryers are two distinct kitchen appliances that offer different cooking methods and outcomes. While both are known for creating crispy and indulgent dishes, they diverge in the way they cook food and the amount of oil required. Deep fat fryers operate by submerging food in a substantial amount of hot oil, resulting in deep frying and achieving that signature golden and crunchy texture. On the other hand, air fryers utilise a different approach, relying on hot air circulation and a minimal quantity of oil to produce similar crispy results. This makes air fryers a healthier alternative as they require significantly less oil, often up to 80% less, compared to deep-fat fryers.

The reduction in oil consumption can lead to lower calorie and fat content in dishes, making them a favourable choice for those seeking a healthier cooking method. Moreover, air fryers offer versatility beyond frying. With their ability to grill, roast, bake, and reheat food, they provide a range of culinary possibilities. This flexibility allows for the creation of a variety of dishes, from crispy vegetables and succulent meats to even desserts. In contrast, deep-fat fryers are primarily designed for frying purposes and may have limited functionality beyond that. The decision between an air fryer and a deep-fat fryer depends on personal preferences, health considerations, and desired cooking versatility. If you aim to achieve the crispy texture of fried food with less oil and a broader range of cooking options, an air fryer may be the ideal choice for you.

How do Airfryers work?

Air fryers cook food using a combination of hot air circulation, radiant heat, and a minimal amount of oil.

Here's a breakdown of the cooking process:

Convection Heating: Air fryers use convection heating, where a heating element located near the food generates hot air.

Rapid Air Circulation: The hot air is rapidly circulated around the food by a high-powered fan, ensuring even heat distribution.

Maillard Reaction: The circulating hot air creates a Maillard reaction on the food's surface, resulting in browning and a crispy texture.

Minimal Oil Application: While air fryers require a small amount of oil, usually just a tablespoon or less, it is used sparingly to enhance flavour and aid in browning.

Cooking Basket: Food is placed in a perforated cooking basket or tray, allowing excess oil and moisture to drain away while the hot air circulates around it.

Cooking Time: Air fryers typically cook food faster than traditional methods due to the efficient heat circulation, reducing cooking times by up to 20%.

Versatile Cooking Methods: In addition to frying, air fryers can grill, roast, bake, and even reheat food, providing versatility in the kitchen.

Healthier Option: Air frying requires significantly less oil compared to deep frying, making it a healthier alternative with reduced calorie and fat content.

By combining these elements, air fryers deliver crispy and delicious results with a fraction of the oil traditionally used in deep frying.

Mastering the Art of Crispy and Healthy Cooking

Achieving perfectly crispy and flavourful results with your air fryer while maintaining the healthiness of your dishes is an art worth mastering.

To ensure that delightful crunch and golden colour, start by preheating your air fryer. This step allows for optimal cooking conditions and helps achieve that coveted crispy texture. Most air fryers have a preheat function, or you can manually set it to the desired temperature and let it warm up for a few minutes before adding your ingredients. Additionally, using a light coating of oil or cooking spray on your ingredients before air frying can enhance the crispiness while keeping the added fat to a minimum. A little goes a long way, so use just enough to lightly coat the surface of your food. You can also use a brush to evenly distribute the oil and ensure a thin and even layer.

Another trick for achieving crispiness is to arrange the food in a single layer. Crowding the air fryer basket can hinder proper air circulation, resulting in uneven cooking and less crispy results. Give each piece of food enough space to breathe, allowing the hot air to circulate and crisp up all sides.

For that extra crunch, consider breading your ingredients with healthier alternatives like whole wheat breadcrumbs or crushed nuts instead of traditional white bread crumbs. These options add texture and flavour while providing additional nutrients. You can also experiment with various seasonings, herbs, and spices to infuse your dishes with tantalising flavours without excessive salt or added calories.

With the air fryer's efficient cooking process, you can achieve crispy and delicious results while significantly reducing the amount of oil traditionally used. The hot circulating air quickly evaporates moisture from the food's surface, creating a crispy exterior. It's a wonderful way to enjoy your favourite fried foods guilt-free.

By mastering the art of crispy and healthy cooking with your air fryer, you can create a wide range of dishes that are both delicious and nutritious. From crispy vegetable medleys to perfectly cooked proteins and even delectable desserts, the air fryer opens up a world of possibilities for healthier cooking options.

So, get ready to embark on a journey of culinary exploration and discover the art of crispy and healthy cooking with your air fryer. Let your creativity soar as you experiment with different ingredients, seasonings, and techniques to create mouthwatering dishes that satisfy both your taste buds and your desire for a healthier lifestyle.

Caring, Maintaining, and Cleaning Your Air Fryer:

Caring, Maintaining, and Cleaning Your Air Fryer

Read the instruction manual: Familiarize yourself with the specific care and maintenance instructions provided by the manufacturer. Different air fryer models may have unique features and requirements.

Regular cleaning: Clean your air fryer after each use to prevent the buildup of grease and food residue. Most air fryers have removable parts that are dishwasher safe. Alternatively, you can hand wash them with warm, soapy water.

Wipe the interior: Use a soft cloth or sponge to wipe the interior of the air fryer. Avoid abrasive cleaners or scouring pads that could damage the non-stick coating.

Be gentle with the basket: The air fryer basket is where most of the cooking takes place. Handle it with care to avoid scratching the non-stick surface. Use wooden or silicone utensils instead of metal ones.

Remove excess grease: After cooking greasy foods, use paper towels or a heat-resistant mat to absorb excess oil from the bottom of the air fryer. This prevents smoking and unpleasant odors during subsequent uses.

Avoid submerging the unit: Air fryers have electrical components that should not be immersed in water. Clean the exterior with a damp cloth, and make sure it's completely dry before using it again.

Prevent odors: If your air fryer develops unpleasant odors, try wiping the interior with a cloth dipped in a mixture of water and lemon juice or vinegar. This helps neutralise any lingering smells.

Check for stuck-on food: If you encounter stubborn food residue, soak the affected parts in warm, soapy water for a while to loosen it. Then gently scrub with a non-abrasive sponge or brush.

Store properly: When not in use, ensure your air fryer is completely cool before storing it. Avoid placing heavy items on top of it, as this could damage the delicate components.

Replace parts as needed: If any parts of your air fryer become damaged or worn out, refer to the manufacturer's guidelines for replacement parts. Properly functioning components ensure optimal performance.

By following these care, maintenance, and cleaning tips, you can prolong the lifespan of your air fryer and ensure its continued efficiency in delivering delicious and healthy meals. Regular maintenance will keep your air fryer in top shape and ready for your next culinary adventure.

Let's Cook!

As we embark on this culinary journey with the air fryer, we hope you feel inspired and excited to explore the endless possibilities it offers. This cookbook is designed to be your trusty companion in the kitchen, guiding you through the art of air frying and unveiling a treasure trove of delicious recipes. From healthy vegetable creations to fast and easy family favourites, and from versatile sauces to mouthwatering dressings, our goal is to provide you with a collection of recipes that celebrate the UK's diverse culinary landscape.

Throughout the pages that follow, you will discover recipes crafted with love and creativity, all tailored to the air fryer's unique cooking capabilities. Each dish has been carefully adapted to deliver the perfect balance of crispiness, flavour, and healthiness. We invite you to bring your favourite traditional recipes to the air fryer and witness the magic of transforming them into wholesome delights that the whole family will enjoy.

So, whether you are an air fryer novice or a seasoned pro, we believe this cookbook will become your go-to resource for creating delectable meals that tick all the boxes of convenience, taste, and nutritional value. Get ready to experience the joy of crispy and healthy cooking like never before.

Now, without further ado, let's dive into the recipes and unlock the full potential of your air fryer. From tantalising appetisers to satisfying main courses and irresistible desserts, each recipe has been thoughtfully curated to provide you with delightful culinary adventures. So, fire up your air fryer, gather your ingredients, and let's embark on a delicious journey that will leave your taste buds longing for more. Happy air frying!

Note: Throughout this cookbook, measurements are presented in UK style, ensuring that you can easily follow along with confidence and precision. Enjoy the convenience, versatility, and flavour-packed results that the air fryer brings to your kitchen.

Happy cooking and bon appétit!

Chapter 1 Breakfast

Beef Burgers

Prep Time: 15 minutes / Cook Time: 10-15 minutes
Serves: 4

Ingredients:

- 500g ground beef
- 1 small onion, finely chopped
- 2 cloves of garlic, minced
- 1 tablespoon Worcestershire sauce
- 1 teaspoon Dijon mustard
- 1 teaspoon salt
- 1/2 teaspoon black pepper
- 4 burger buns
- Lettuce leaves, tomato slices, and pickles (optional, for serving)

Instructions:

1. In a mixing bowl, combine the ground beef, chopped onion, minced garlic, Worcestershire sauce, Dijon mustard, salt, and black pepper. Mix well until all the ingredients are evenly incorporated.
2. Divide the mixture into 4 equal portions and shape them into patties, about 1/2 to 3/4 inch thick. Make a slight indentation in the centre of each patty with your thumb to prevent it from puffing up while cooking.
3. Preheat the air fryer under medium-high heat.
4. Place the burger patties on the air fryer. Cook for about 4-5 minutes on each side for medium doneness, or adjust the cooking time based on your desired level of doneness.
5. While the burgers are cooking, you can lightly toast the burger buns if desired.
6. Once the burgers are cooked to your liking, remove them from the air fryer and let them rest for a few minutes.
7. Assemble the burgers by placing each patty on a toasted bun. Add lettuce leaves, tomato slices, and pickles if desired. You can also add additional toppings such as cheese, bacon, or condiments like ketchup or mayonnaise.
8. Serve the beef burgers hot and enjoy!

Chicken Katsu Curry

Prep Time: 20 minutes / Cook Time: 30 minutes
Serves: 4

Ingredients:

For the Chicken Katsu:
- 4 boneless, skinless chicken breasts
- Salt and pepper, to taste
- 80g all-purpose flour
- 2 eggs, beaten
- 150g panko breadcrumbs
- Vegetable oil, for frying

For the Curry Sauce:
- 1 onion, finely chopped
- 2 carrots, peeled and diced
- 2 potatoes, peeled and diced
- 2 cloves of garlic, minced
- 1 tablespoon curry powder
- 1 tablespoon vegetable oil
- 500ml chicken or vegetable broth
- 200ml coconut milk
- 1 tablespoon soy sauce
- 1 tablespoon honey
- Salt and pepper, to taste

For Serving:
- Cooked rice
- Pickled ginger (optional)
- Chopped spring onions (optional)

Instructions:

1. Start by preparing the chicken katsu. Season the chicken breasts with salt and pepper on both sides.
2. Place the flour, beaten eggs, and panko breadcrumbs into three separate shallow bowls.
3. Dredge each chicken breast in the flour, shaking off any excess. Dip the floured chicken into the beaten eggs, allowing any excess to drip off, and then coat it with the panko breadcrumbs, pressing lightly to adhere.
4. Heat vegetable oil in a large pan over medium-high heat. Fry the breaded chicken breasts for about 4-5 minutes on each side or until golden brown and cooked through. Transfer the cooked chicken to a paper towel-lined plate to drain excess oil. Set aside.
5. In a separate saucepan, heat 1 tablespoon of vegetable oil over medium heat. Add the chopped onion and minced garlic, and cook until the onion becomes translucent.
6. Add the diced carrots and potatoes to the pan and cook for another 5 minutes.
7. Sprinkle the curry powder over the vegetables and stir well to coat.
8. Pour in the chicken or vegetable broth and bring the mixture to a simmer. Cook for about 15 minutes or until the vegetables are tender.
9. Stir in the coconut milk, soy sauce, and honey. Season with salt and pepper to taste. Simmer for an additional 5 minutes to allow the flavours to meld together.

10. Using a blender or immersion blender, puree the curry sauce until smooth. If needed, return the sauce to the pan and heat it gently.
11. To serve, slice the chicken katsu into strips. Place a scoop of cooked rice on each plate, top with the chicken katsu, and pour the curry sauce over the chicken. Garnish with pickled ginger and chopped spring onions, if desired.
12. Enjoy your delicious Chicken Katsu Curry!

Garlic Prawns

Prep Time: 10 minutes / Cook Time: 10 minutes
Serves: 4

Ingredients:

- 500g large prawns, peeled and deveined
- 4 cloves of garlic, minced
- 2 tablespoons butter
- 2 tablespoons olive oil
- 1 tablespoon lemon juice
- 1 tablespoon chopped fresh parsley
- Salt and pepper, to taste
- Lemon wedges, for serving

Instructions:

1. Rinse the prawns under cold water and pat them dry with paper towels. Season the prawns with salt and pepper.
2. In a large skillet, heat the butter and olive oil over medium heat until the butter has melted.
3. Add the minced garlic to the skillet and Sauté for about 1 minute until fragrant. Be careful not to let the garlic burn.
4. Increase the heat to medium-high and add the seasoned prawns to the skillet. Cook for about 2-3 minutes on each side until they turn pink and opaque. The cooking time may vary depending on the size of the prawns.
5. Drizzle the lemon juice over the prawns and sprinkle with chopped parsley. Toss the prawns in the garlic butter sauce to coat evenly.
6. Remove the skillet from the heat and let the prawns rest for a minute.
7. Serve the garlic prawns hot with lemon wedges on the side for squeezing over the prawns.
8. You can enjoy the garlic prawns as an appetiser, serve them over pasta, or as a main course with a side of vegetables or salad.
9. Enjoy the delicious Garlic Prawns!

Corn on the Cob

Prep Time: 5 minutes / Cook Time: 10-15 minutes
Serves: 4

Ingredients:

- 4 ears of corn, husked
- Water, for boiling
- Butter, for serving
- Salt and pepper, to taste

Instructions:

1. Fill a large pot with water and bring it to a boil.
2. Once the water is boiling, carefully add the ears of corn to the pot. Make sure the corn is fully submerged in the water.
3. Boil the corn for 10-15 minutes or until it becomes tender. The cooking time may vary depending on the size and freshness of the corn.
4. While the corn is boiling, prepare a bowl of cold water and set it aside.
5. Once the corn is cooked, use tongs to remove the ears from the pot and transfer them immediately to the bowl of cold water. This helps to stop the cooking process and cools down the corn.
6. Drain the corn and pat it dry with a paper towel.
7. Serve the corn on the cob with butter, salt, and pepper. You can spread butter over the warm corn and season it with salt and pepper according to your taste.
8. Enjoy the delicious Corn on the Cob as a side dish or as part of a barbecue or summer meal!

Halloumi Fries

Prep Time: 10 minutes / Cook Time: 10 minutes
Serves: 4

Ingredients:

- 250g halloumi cheese
- 60g all-purpose flour
- 2 tablespoons paprika
- 1 teaspoon garlic powder
- Vegetable oil, for frying
- Lemon wedges, for serving
- Fresh parsley, for garnish (optional)

Instructions:

1. Cut the halloumi cheese into fries-shaped strips, about 1 cm thick.
2. In a shallow bowl, combine the flour, paprika, and garlic powder. Mix well to evenly distribute the spices.
3. Roll each halloumi strip in the seasoned flour mixture, making sure all sides are coated. Shake off any excess flour.
4. In a deep frying pan or saucepan, heat enough vegetable oil to cover the halloumi fries over medium-high heat.
5. Carefully place the coated halloumi fries into the hot oil, working in batches to avoid overcrowding the pan.
6. Fry the halloumi fries for about 2-3 minutes on each side, or until they turn golden brown and crispy.
7. Once the fries are cooked to your liking, use a slotted

spoon or tongs to transfer them to a paper towel-lined plate to drain excess oil.

8. Repeat the frying process with the remaining halloumi fries until all are cooked.

9. Serve the halloumi fries hot, accompanied by lemon wedges for squeezing over the fries. You can also garnish them with fresh parsley, if desired.

10. Halloumi fries are best enjoyed immediately while they are still warm and crispy.

11. Dip the halloumi fries into your favourite sauce or enjoy them as is.

12. Enjoy the delicious Halloumi Fries as a tasty appetiser or snack!

Pumpkin Spice Pancakes With Maple Syrup

Prep Time: 10 minutes / Cook time: 20 minutes
Serves: 4

Ingredients:
- 180g all-purpose flour
- 25g granulated sugar
- 15g baking powder
- 5g pumpkin pie spice
- 2.5g salt
- 240ml milk
- 180g pumpkin puree
- 1 large egg
- 30g melted butter
- 5ml vanilla extract
- Maple syrup, for serving
- Optional toppings: whipped cream, chopped nuts, or cinnamon

Instructions:
1. In a large bowl, whisk together the flour, granulated sugar, baking powder, pumpkin pie spice, and salt.

2. In a separate bowl, whisk together the milk, pumpkin puree, egg, melted butter, and vanilla extract until well combined.

3. Pour the wet ingredients into the dry ingredients and stir until just combined. Do not overmix; a few lumps are okay.

4. Heat a non-stick skillet or griddle over medium heat. Lightly grease the surface with butter or cooking spray.

5. Scoop about 60ml of batter onto the skillet for each pancake. Cook until bubbles form on the surface, then flip and cook the other side until golden brown.

6. Transfer the cooked pancakes to a plate and keep warm. Repeat with the remaining batter, greasing the skillet as needed.

7. Serve the pumpkin spice pancakes with maple syrup and any desired toppings, such as whipped cream, chopped nuts, or a sprinkle of cinnamon.

Garlic Bread

Prep Time: 10 minutes / Cook Time: 15 minutes
Serves: 4-6

Ingredients:
- 1 French baguette or loaf of Italian bread
- 113g unsalted butter, softened
- 4 cloves of garlic, minced
- 2 tablespoons fresh parsley, finely chopped
- 1/4 teaspoon salt
- 1/4 teaspoon black pepper

Instructions:
1. Preheat the air fryer oven to 180°C.

2. Slice the baguette or Italian bread loaf lengthwise, creating two halves.

3. In a small bowl, combine the softened butter, minced garlic, chopped parsley, salt, and black pepper. Mix well until all the ingredients are evenly incorporated.

4. Spread the garlic butter mixture evenly on the cut sides of the bread.

5. Place the buttered bread halves on a baking sheet or directly on the air fryer oven rack.

6. Bake in the preheated air fryer oven for about 10-15 minutes or until the bread is crispy on the outside and lightly golden.

7. Remove the garlic bread from the air fryer oven and let it cool for a few minutes.

8. Slice the garlic bread into individual servings and serve warm.

9. Garlic bread pairs well with pasta dishes, soups, salads, or can be enjoyed on its own as a delicious appetiser or side dish.

Vegemite On Toast

Prep Time: 2 minutes / Cook time: 2 minutes
Serves: 1

Ingredients:
- 2 slices of bread (white or whole wheat)
- Butter, softened
- Vegemite

Instructions:
1. Toast the bread slices to your desired level of doneness.

2. Spread a thin layer of butter on each slice of toast. This step is optional but adds richness to the flavour.

3. Take a small amount of Vegemite (start with a small quantity as it has a strong flavour) and spread it evenly on top of the buttered toast.

4. If preferred, you can cut the toast into halves or quarters for easier handling.

5. Serve the Vegemite toast immediately while it's still warm.

Cheeseburger Spring Rolls

Prep Time: 30 minutes / Cook Time: 10 minutes
Serves: 4-6

Ingredients:

- 250g ground beef
- 1 small onion, finely chopped
- 2 cloves of garlic, minced
- 1 tablespoon Worcestershire sauce
- 1 tablespoon ketchup
- Salt and pepper, to taste
- 8-10 spring roll wrappers
- 150g cheddar cheese, shredded
- Vegetable oil, for frying
- Ketchup or your favourite dipping sauce, for serving

Instructions:

1. In a pan, heat a small amount of vegetable oil over medium heat. Add the chopped onion and minced garlic, and Sauté until the onion becomes translucent.
2. Add the ground beef to the pan and cook until browned, breaking it up into small pieces with a spatula or spoon.
3. Stir in the Worcestershire sauce, ketchup, salt, and pepper. Cook for an additional 2-3 minutes, allowing the flavours to meld. Remove from heat and let the filling cool slightly.
4. Place a spring roll wrapper on a clean surface, positioning it in a diamond shape with one point facing towards you.
5. Spoon a small amount of the beef filling onto the bottom centre of the wrapper, leaving a border of about 2 cm around the edges.
6. Sprinkle a generous amount of shredded cheddar cheese over the beef filling.
7. Fold the bottom point of the wrapper over the filling, tucking it tightly. Fold in the left and right points towards the centre, forming a tight envelope. Roll the spring roll away from you, sealing the edges with a bit of water to secure.
8. Repeat the process with the remaining spring roll wrappers and filling.
9. In a deep pan or fryer, heat vegetable oil to approximately 180° for deep frying.
10. Carefully place the cheeseburger spring rolls into the hot oil, frying them in batches to avoid overcrowding the pan. Fry for about 3-4 minutes or until they turn golden brown and crispy.
11. Use a slotted spoon or tongs to remove the spring rolls from the oil and transfer them to a paper towel-lined plate to drain excess oil.
12. Serve the cheeseburger spring rolls hot with ketchup or your favourite dipping sauce on the side.
13. Enjoy these delicious cheeseburger spring rolls as a unique and flavourful appetiser or snack!

caramelised Onion Tart

Prep Time: 20 minutes / Cook Time: 1 hour
Serves: 4-6

Ingredients:

For the Tart Crust:
- 200g all-purpose flour
- 100g unsalted butter, cold and cubed
- 1/2 teaspoon salt
- 3-4 tablespoons ice-cold water

For the caramelised Onions:
- 4 large onions, thinly sliced
- 2 tablespoons unsalted butter
- 2 tablespoons olive oil
- 1 tablespoon brown sugar
- 1 tablespoon balsamic vinegar
- Salt and pepper, to taste

For the Filling:
- 150g Gruyere cheese, grated
- 2 eggs
- 200ml heavy cream
- 1/4 teaspoon nutmeg
- Salt and pepper, to taste

Instructions:

1. Preheat the air fryer oven to 180°C.
2. In a food processor, combine the flour, cold cubed butter, and salt. Pulse until the mixture resembles coarse crumbs.
3. Gradually add the ice-cold water, one tablespoon at a time, pulsing after each addition, until the dough comes together. Be careful not to overmix.
4. Transfer the dough onto a lightly floured surface and shape it into a ball. Wrap it in plastic wrap and refrigerate for 30 minutes.
5. Meanwhile, prepare the caramelised onions. In a large pan, melt the butter and olive oil over medium heat. Add the thinly sliced onions and cook, stirring occasionally, until they become soft and golden brown, about 30 minutes.
6. Stir in the brown sugar and balsamic vinegar, and continue cooking for an additional 5 minutes. Season with salt and pepper to taste. Remove from heat and set aside.
7. Roll out the chilled tart dough on a lightly floured surface to fit a 9-inch tart pan. Press the dough into the pan, trimming any excess.
8. In a bowl, whisk together the eggs, heavy cream, nutmeg, salt, and pepper.
9. Sprinkle the grated Gruyere cheese over the tart crust. Spread the caramelised onions evenly over the cheese.
10. Pour the egg and cream mixture over the onions, ensuring it fills the tart evenly.
11. Place the tart pan on a baking sheet and bake in the preheated air fryer oven for about 30-35 minutes, or

until the filling is set and the crust is golden brown.

12. Remove the caramelised onion tart from the air fryer oven and let it cool slightly before slicing.

13. Serve the tart warm or at room temperature as a delicious appetiser or main course. It pairs well with a fresh salad or roasted vegetables.

Chicken and Chorizo Paella

Prep Time: 15 minutes / Cook Time: 40 minutes
Serves: 4-6

Ingredients:

- 2 tablespoons olive oil
- 4 boneless, skinless chicken thighs, cut into bite-sized pieces
- 150g chorizo sausage, sliced
- 1 onion, finely chopped
- 2 cloves of garlic, minced
- 1 red bell pepper, diced
- 200g paella rice (short-grain rice)
- 1 teaspoon smoked paprika
- 1/2 teaspoon saffron threads (optional)
- 400ml chicken broth
- 400ml canned diced tomatoes
- 200g frozen peas
- Salt and pepper, to taste
- Lemon wedges, for serving
- Fresh parsley, chopped, for garnish

Instructions:

1. In a large paella pan or a wide, shallow skillet, heat the olive oil over medium heat.

2. Add the chicken pieces to the pan and cook until browned on all sides. Remove the chicken from the pan and set aside.

3. In the same pan, add the sliced chorizo sausage and cook until it starts to release its oils and becomes slightly crispy. Remove the chorizo from the pan and set aside with the chicken.

4. In the same pan, add the chopped onion, minced garlic, and diced red bell pepper. Sauté until the vegetables become tender and fragrant.

5. Add the paella rice to the pan and stir to coat it with the oil and vegetables. Cook for a minute or two until the rice grains start to become translucent.

6. Sprinkle the smoked paprika and saffron threads (if using) over the rice, stirring well to distribute the flavours.

7. Pour in the chicken broth and diced tomatoes, stirring to combine. Season with salt and pepper to taste.

8. Return the browned chicken and chorizo to the pan, nestling them into the rice mixture. Bring the liquid to a simmer.

9. Cover the pan with a lid or aluminium foil and reduce the heat to low. Let the paella simmer for about 20-25 minutes or until the rice is cooked and has absorbed most of the liquid.

10. Remove the lid and scatter the frozen peas over the top of the paella. Cover again and cook for an additional 5 minutes until the peas are heated through.

11. Once cooked, remove the paella from the heat and let it rest, covered, for a few minutes.

12. Serve the chicken and chorizo paella hot, garnished with fresh parsley and accompanied by lemon wedges for squeezing over the rice.

Greek Yoghourt Pancakes With Delicious Blueberry Compote

Prep Time: 10 minutes / Cook time: 15 minutes
Serves: 4

Ingredients for Greek Yoghourt Pancakes:

- 180g all-purpose flour
- 25g granulated sugar
- 5g baking powder
2.5g baking soda
- 2g salt
- 240g Greek yoghourt
- 120ml milk
- 2 large eggs
- 5ml vanilla extract
- Butter or oil for greasing the pan

Ingredients for Blueberry Compote:

- 300g blueberries (fresh or frozen)
- 60ml water
- 30ml maple syrup (or more to taste)
- 15ml lemon juice
- Optional toppings: Greek yoghourt, additional blueberries, and maple syrup

Instructions:

1. In a large bowl, whisk together the flour, sugar, baking powder, baking soda, and salt.

2. In a separate bowl, whisk together the Greek yoghourt, milk, eggs, and vanilla extract until smooth.

3. Pour the wet ingredients into the dry ingredients and stir until just combined. The batter may be thick; avoid overmixing.

4. Preheat a non-stick skillet or griddle over medium heat. Grease the surface with butter or oil.

5. Using a 60 ml measuring cup, pour the pancake batter onto the skillet. Cook until bubbles form on the surface, then flip and cook the other side until golden brown. Repeat with the remaining batter.

6. For the blueberry compote, combine the blueberries, water, maple syrup, and lemon juice in a small saucepan. Bring to a simmer over medium heat and cook for about 5-7 minutes until the blueberries soften and release their juices. Stir occasionally and gently mash some of the blueberries with the back of

a spoon to thicken the compote.

7. Serve the Greek yoghourt pancakes with the blueberry compote on top. You can also add a dollop of Greek yoghourt, additional blueberries, and a drizzle of maple syrup if desired.

Mediterranean Fish Parcels

Prep Time: 15 minutes / Cook Time: 20 minutes
Serves: 4

Ingredients:

- 4 white fish fillets (such as cod, haddock, or sea bass)
- 1 red bell pepper, thinly sliced
- 1 yellow bell pepper, thinly sliced
- 1 small red onion, thinly sliced
- 1 small zucchini, thinly sliced
- 8 cherry tomatoes, halved
- 2 cloves of garlic, minced
- 2 tablespoons olive oil
- Juice of 1 lemon
- 1 teaspoon dried oregano
- Salt and pepper, to taste
- Fresh parsley, chopped, for garnish
- Lemon wedges, for serving

Instructions:

1. Preheat the air fryer oven to 200°C.
2. Cut four large squares of parchment paper or aluminium foil, approximately 30 cm (12 inches) in size.
3. Place a fish fillet in the centre of each parchment square.
4. In a bowl, combine the sliced red and yellow bell peppers, red onion, zucchini, cherry tomatoes, minced garlic, olive oil, lemon juice, dried oregano, salt, and pepper. Toss the vegetables to coat them evenly with the seasoning.
5. Divide the vegetable mixture equally among the fish fillets, spooning it on top of each fillet.
6. Fold the parchment paper or foil over the fish and vegetables, then tightly seal the edges to create a packet.
7. Place the fish parcels on a baking sheet and transfer them to the preheated air fryer oven.
8. Bake for approximately 15-20 minutes, or until the fish is cooked through and flakes easily with a fork.
9. Carefully open the parcels, taking caution of the hot steam. Transfer the fish and vegetables onto serving plates.
10. Sprinkle with fresh chopped parsley for garnish.
11. Serve the Mediterranean fish parcels hot, accompanied by lemon wedges on the side.

Smashed Avocado and Bacon on Toast

Prep Time: 10 minutes / Cook Time: 10 minutes
Serves: 2

Ingredients:

- 4 slices of bread (your choice of bread)
- 2 ripe avocados
- Juice of 1/2 lemon
- Salt and pepper, to taste
- 4 slices of cooked bacon
- Fresh cilantro or parsley, chopped, for garnish (optional)

Instructions:

1. Toast the bread slices until golden brown and crispy. Set aside.
2. Cut the avocados in half and remove the pits. Scoop the avocado flesh into a bowl.
3. Add the lemon juice, salt, and pepper to the avocado. Mash the avocado with a fork until you reach your desired consistency. You can leave it slightly chunky or make it smoother.
4. Heat a skillet over medium heat and add the cooked bacon slices. Cook the bacon until crispy on both sides. Remove from the skillet and place on a paper towel to drain excess grease. Once cooled, break the bacon slices in half.
5. Spread a generous amount of the smashed avocado onto each slice of toasted bread.
6. Top each slice of bread with 2 bacon halves.
7. Sprinkle with fresh chopped cilantro or parsley for added flavour and garnish.
8. Serve the smashed avocado and bacon on toast as a delicious and satisfying breakfast or brunch option.

Chicken and Sweetcorn Soup

Prep Time: 15 minutes / Cook Time: 25 minutes
Serves: 4

Ingredients:

- 250g boneless, skinless chicken breasts, thinly sliced
- 15ml vegetable oil
- 1 small onion, finely chopped
- 2 cloves of garlic, minced
- 5g grated ginger
- 480ml chicken broth
- 240ml water
- 150g sweetcorn kernels (fresh or frozen)
- 100g sliced mushrooms
- 30ml soy sauce
- 15g cornstarch (cornflour)
- 2 eggs, lightly beaten
- Salt and pepper, to taste
- Spring onions, thinly sliced, for garnish

Instructions:

1. In a large pot or saucepan, heat the vegetable oil over medium heat.
2. Add the sliced chicken breasts to the pot and cook until they are no longer pink. Remove the chicken from the pot and set aside.
3. In the same pot, add the chopped onion, minced garlic, and grated ginger. Sauté until the onion becomes translucent and fragrant.
4. Pour in the chicken broth and water, and bring the liquid to a simmer.
5. Add the sweetcorn kernels and sliced mushrooms to the pot. Let the soup simmer for about 10 minutes, allowing the flavours to meld together.
6. In a small bowl, mix the soy sauce and cornstarch to create a slurry. Stir until the cornstarch is fully dissolved.
7. Slowly pour the slurry into the simmering soup, stirring continuously. This will help thicken the soup slightly.
8. Return the cooked chicken to the pot and simmer for an additional 5 minutes to ensure the chicken is heated through.
9. While gently stirring the soup in a circular motion, slowly pour the beaten eggs into the pot. The eggs will create delicate ribbons in the soup.
10. Season the soup with salt and pepper to taste. Adjust the seasoning according to your preference.
11. Ladle the chicken and sweetcorn soup into serving bowls.
12. Garnish with thinly sliced spring onions for added freshness and flavour.
13. Serve the chicken and sweetcorn soup hot as a comforting and nutritious meal.

Air Fryer Glazed Bacon Recipe

Prep Time: 5 minutes / Cook Time: 10 minutes
Serves: 2

Ingredients

- 8 slices of bacon
- 2 tablespoons brown sugar
- 1 tablespoon maple syrup
- 1 teaspoon Dijon mustard
- Salt and pepper, to taste

Instructions

1. Preheat the air fryer to 400°F (200°C).
2. In a small bowl, mix together the brown sugar, maple syrup, Dijon mustard, salt, and pepper to create the glaze.
3. Place the bacon slices in a single layer in the air fryer basket. Spray the basket with a non stick cooking spray or use a specific air fryer liner to prevent the bacon from sticking to the basket.

4. Brush the glaze evenly over the bacon slices. For this step you can use a pastry brush or a silicon glazing brush.
5. Cook the bacon for 7-10 minutes, or until crispy and glaze has caramelised. For extra crispy bacon you can add an extra minute or two to the cooking time.
6. Remove the bacon from the air fryer and place it on a paper towel to drain. Pat the top of the bacon dry with another paper towel.
7. Serve immediately and enjoy!

Air Fryer Breakfast Tostadas Recipe

Prep Time: 5 minutes / Cook Time: 10-15 minutes
Serves:4

Ingredients

- 4 corn tortillas
- 300 g black beans, drained and rinsed
- 300 g shredded cheddar cheese
- 4 large eggs
- Salt and pepper, to taste
- Salsa, avocado, hot sauce, and cilantro, for serving (optional)

Instructions

1. Preheat the air fryer to 400°F (200°C).
2. Place the tortillas in a single layer in the air fryer basket. Then you can spray them with a butter flavoured cooking spray.
3. Cook the tortillas for 2-3 minutes, or until crispy and lightly golden.
4. Remove the tortillas from the air fryer and set aside.
5. In a bowl, mash the black beans with a fork.
6. Spread a layer of mashed black beans on each tortilla, followed by a sprinkle of shredded cheese.
7. In another bowl, whisk together the eggs, salt, and pepper.
8. Pour the egg mixture into the air fryer basket and cook for 5-7 minutes, or until fully cooked.
9. Place the cooked eggs on top of the cheese and black beans on each tortilla.
10. Return the tostadas to the air fryer and cook for an additional 2-3 minutes, or until the cheese is melted.
11. Serve the tostadas immediately with salsa, avocado, hot sauce, and cilantro, if desired.
12. Enjoy this tasty and easy air fryer breakfast tostada recipe!.

Breakfast Quesadilla Recipe

Prep Time: 10 minutes / Cook Time: 10-12 minutes
Serves: 4

Ingredients:

- 4 large flour tortillas
- 4 large eggs, beaten
- 60 ml milk

- Salt and pepper, to taste
- 227 g shredded cheddar cheese
- 227 g diced cooked minced beef
- Salsa, for serving (optional)
- Avocado, for serving (optional)
- Sour cream, for serving (optional)

Instructions:

1. Preheat the air fryer to 400°F (200°C).
2. In a large bowl, whisk together the eggs, milk, salt, and pepper until well combined.
3. In a large nonstick skillet over medium heat, cook the egg mixture, stirring occasionally, until fully cooked and scrambled. Remove from heat.
4. Place a tortilla on a large cutting board. Spread 1/4 of the shredded cheese evenly over half of the tortilla.
5. Spoon 1/4 of the scrambled eggs over the cheese, then sprinkle 1/4 of the cooked minced beef over the eggs.
6. Fold the other half of the tortilla over the filling to create a half-moon shape. Repeat with the remaining tortillas to make 4 quesadillas.
7. Place the quesadillas in the air fryer basket in a single layer.
8. Cook the quesadillas for 6-8 minutes, or until the cheese is melted and the tortillas are crispy and golden brown.
9. Serve the breakfast quesadillas immediately with salsa, avocado, and sour cream, if desired.

Air Fryer Hashbrowns Recipe

Prep Time: 10 minutes / Cook Time: 10-15 minutes
Serves: 4

Ingredients:

- 500 g grated potatoes
- 2 tbsp olive oil
- 1 tsp onion powder
- Salt and pepper, to taste
- 50 g shredded cheddar cheese (optional)

Instructions:

1. Preheat the air fryer to 400°F (200°C).
2. In a large bowl, mix together the grated potatoes, olive oil, onion powder, salt, and pepper.
3. Place spoonfuls of the potato mixture into the air fryer basket, pressing down slightly to form compact patties.

4. Cook the hash browns for 10-15 minutes, or until they are crispy and golden brown, flipping them once during cooking.
5. If desired, sprinkle the shredded cheddar cheese over the hash browns during the last 2-3 minutes of cooking, until the cheese is melted.
6. Serve the hash browns immediately, topped with chopped fresh parsley or chives, if desired.

Breakfast Waffles Recipe

Prep Time: 5-10 minutes / Cook Time: 5 minutes
Serves: 4

Ingredients:

- 188 g all-purpose flour
- 2 tsp baking powder
- 1/2 tsp salt
- 1 tbsp granulated sugar
- 420 ml milk
- 2 large eggs
- 113 g unsalted butter, melted
- 1 tsp vanilla extract

Non-stick cooking spray or butter, for greasing the air fryer basket

Instructions:

1. In a medium bowl, whisk together the flour, baking powder, salt, and sugar.
2. In a separate bowl, whisk together the milk, eggs, melted butter, and vanilla extract.
3. Add the wet ingredients to the dry ingredients and whisk until just combined (a few lumps are okay).
4. Preheat the air fryer to 375°F (190°C).
5. Lightly grease the air fryer basket with non-stick cooking spray or butter.
6. Pour 60 ml of the batter into the centre of the air fryer basket, spreading it out slightly to the edges.
7. Cook the waffle for 4-5 minutes, or until it is golden brown and cooked through.
8. Using a spatula, carefully remove the waffle from the air fryer basket and transfer it to a plate.
9. Repeat with the remaining batter, lightly greasing the basket before each batch.
10. Serve the waffles hot, topped with your favourite toppings such as fresh fruit, syrup, or whipped cream.

Chapter 2 Main Recipes

Beef Stir-Fry with Noodles

Prep Time: 15 minutes / Cook Time: 15 minutes
Serves: 4

Ingredients:
- 300g beef sirloin or flank steak, thinly sliced
- 200g dried egg noodles
- 2 tablespoons vegetable oil
- 2 cloves of garlic, minced
- 1 red bell pepper, thinly sliced
- 1 yellow bell pepper, thinly sliced
- 1 small onion, thinly sliced
- 100g sugar snap peas, trimmed
- 2 tablespoons soy sauce
- 1 tablespoon oyster sauce
- 1 tablespoon hoisin sauce
- 1 tablespoon sesame oil
- 1 teaspoon cornstarch (cornflour)
- Salt and pepper, to taste
- Fresh cilantro or spring onions, chopped, for garnish (optional)

Instructions:
1. Cook the dried egg noodles according to the package instructions until al dente. Drain and set aside.
2. In a small bowl, mix together the soy sauce, oyster sauce, hoisin sauce, sesame oil, and cornstarch. Set aside.
3. Heat the vegetable oil in a large pan or wok over high heat.
4. Add the minced garlic and Sauté for a few seconds until fragrant.
5. Add the beef slices to the pan and stir-fry for 2-3 minutes until browned. Remove the beef from the pan and set aside.
6. In the same pan, add the sliced bell peppers, onion, and sugar snap peas. Stir-fry for about 3-4 minutes until the vegetables are crisp-tender.
7. Return the beef to the pan and pour in the sauce mixture. Stir well to coat the beef and vegetables.
8. Add the cooked egg noodles to the pan and toss everything together until well combined. Cook for an additional 2-3 minutes to heat through.
9. Taste the stir-fry and season with salt and pepper as needed.
10. Transfer the beef stir-fry with noodles to serving plates or bowls.
11. Garnish with fresh chopped cilantro or spring onions, if desired.
12. Serve the beef stir-fry with noodles hot and enjoy the flavourful combination of tender beef, vibrant vegetables, and noodles.

Cajun Spiced Shrimp with Rice

Prep Time: 10 minutes / Cook time: 20 minutes
Serves: 4

Ingredients:
- 500 grams shrimp, peeled and deveined
- 2 tablespoons Cajun seasoning
- 2 tablespoons olive oil
- 1 onion, diced
- 2 bell peppers (any colour), diced
- 3 cloves garlic, minced
- 400 grams diced tomatoes
- 240ml chicken or vegetable broth
- 180g long-grain rice
- Salt and pepper to taste
- Fresh parsley, chopped (for garnish)

Instructions:
1. In a bowl, toss the shrimp with the Cajun seasoning until evenly coated. Set aside.
2. In a large skillet or frying pan, heat the olive oil over medium heat. Add the onion, bell peppers, and garlic. Sauté for 5-7 minutes until the vegetables are softened.
3. Add the seasoned shrimp to the skillet and cook for 2-3 minutes per side until they turn pink and opaque. Remove the shrimp from the skillet and set aside.
4. In the same skillet, add the diced tomatoes (with their juices), chicken or vegetable broth, and rice. Season with salt and pepper to taste. Stir well to combine.
5. Bring the mixture to a boil, then reduce the heat to low. Cover the skillet and let the rice cook for about 15-18 minutes, or until it is tender and the liquid is absorbed.
6. Once the rice is cooked, return the cooked shrimp to the skillet and stir to combine with the rice and vegetables. Cook for an additional 1-2 minutes to heat the shrimp through.
7. Remove from heat and garnish with freshly chopped parsley.
8. Serve the Cajun spiced shrimp with rice hot and enjoy!

Pork Chops with Mustard Sauce

Prep Time: 10 minutes / Cook Time: 20 minutes
Serves: 4

Ingredients:
- 4 pork chops
- Salt and pepper, to taste
- 2 tablespoons olive oil
- 2 cloves of garlic, minced

- 1 tablespoon Dijon mustard
- 1 tablespoon whole grain mustard
- 240ml heavy cream
- 2 tablespoons fresh parsley, chopped, for garnish (optional)

Instructions:

1. Season the pork chops with salt and pepper on both sides.
2. Heat the olive oil in a large skillet over medium-high heat.
3. Add the pork chops to the skillet and cook for about 4-5 minutes on each side, or until they reach an internal temperature of 63°C. Adjust the cooking time based on the thickness of the pork chops.
4. Once cooked, transfer the pork chops to a plate and cover with foil to keep warm.
5. In the same skillet, reduce the heat to medium and add the minced garlic. Sauté for about 1 minute until fragrant.
6. Add the Dijon mustard and whole grain mustard to the skillet, stirring to combine with the garlic.
7. Pour in the heavy cream and bring the mixture to a gentle simmer. Allow it to simmer for about 3-4 minutes until the sauce thickens slightly.
8. Return the pork chops to the skillet and coat them with the mustard sauce. Cook for an additional 1-2 minutes to heat the pork chops through.
9. Remove the skillet from the heat.
10. Sprinkle the pork chops with fresh chopped parsley for garnish, if desired.
11. Serve the pork chops with mustard sauce hot alongside your favourite side dishes such as mashed potatoes or roasted vegetables.

Salmon with Dill Sauce

Prep Time: 10 minutes / Cook Time: 15 minutes
Serves: 4

Ingredients:

- 4 salmon fillets (about 150g each)
- Salt and pepper, to taste
- 2 tablespoons olive oil
- 2 tablespoons fresh dill, chopped
- 2 tablespoons lemon juice
- 120ml sour cream
- 1 tablespoon Dijon mustard
- 1 tablespoon honey
- Lemon wedges, for serving
- Fresh dill sprigs, for garnish (optional)

Instructions:

1. Preheat the air fryer oven to 200°C.
2. Season the salmon fillets with salt and pepper on both sides.
3. In a small bowl, combine the olive oil, chopped dill, and lemon juice. Mix well.
4. Place the salmon fillets on a baking sheet lined with

parchment paper.
5. Brush the dill and lemon mixture over the salmon fillets, coating them evenly.
6. Bake the salmon in the preheated air fryer oven for about 12-15 minutes, or until the fish flakes easily with a fork and is cooked to your desired doneness.
7. While the salmon is baking, prepare the dill sauce. In a bowl, mix together the sour cream, Dijon mustard, and honey until well combined.
8. Stir in the chopped fresh dill and season with salt and pepper to taste.
9. Remove the salmon from the air fryer oven and let it rest for a few minutes.
10. Serve the salmon fillets with a dollop of the dill sauce on top.
11. Garnish with fresh dill sprigs, if desired.
12. Serve the salmon with dill sauce hot, accompanied by lemon wedges for squeezing over the fish.

Vegetarian Enchiladas

Prep Time: 20 minutes / Cook time: 30 minutes
Serves: 4

Ingredients:

- 8 tortillas (corn or flour)
- 15ml olive oil
- 1 onion, diced
- 2 bell peppers (any colour), diced
- 2 cloves garlic, minced
- 1 zucchini, diced
- 150g corn kernels (fresh or frozen)
- 240g black beans, rinsed and drained
- 400g diced tomatoes
- 5g ground cumin
- 5g chilli powder
- Salt and pepper to taste
- 100g shredded cheese (cheddar, Monterey Jack, or a blend)
- Fresh cilantro, chopped (for garnish)
- Sour cream, salsa, and guacamole (optional, for serving)

Instructions:

1. Preheat your oven to 180°C. Grease a baking dish and set aside.
2. In a large skillet, heat the olive oil over medium heat. Add the onion, bell peppers, and garlic. Sauté for 5-7 minutes until the vegetables are softened.
3. Add the zucchini, corn kernels, black beans, diced tomatoes (with their juices), ground cumin, chilli powder, salt, and pepper to the skillet. Stir well to combine. Cook for another 5 minutes, allowing the flavours to meld together. Remove from heat.
4. Warm the tortillas in a microwave or on a dry skillet for a few seconds to make them pliable.
5. Place a spoonful of the vegetable mixture onto each

tortilla. Roll it up tightly and place it seam-side down in the greased baking dish. Repeat with the remaining tortillas and filling.

6. Sprinkle the shredded cheese over the enchiladas in the baking dish.

7. Bake in the preheated oven for 20 minutes, or until the cheese is melted and bubbly.

8. Remove from the oven and garnish with freshly chopped cilantro.

9. Serve the vegetarian enchiladas hot, with optional toppings such as sour cream, salsa, and guacamole.

Chicken and Mushroom Tagliatelle

Prep Time: 15 minutes / Cook Time: 25 minutes
Serves: 4

Ingredients:

- 300g tagliatelle pasta
- 2 tablespoons olive oil
- 2 chicken breasts, boneless and skinless, cut into thin strips
- Salt and pepper, to taste
- 200g mushrooms, sliced
- 2 cloves of garlic, minced
- 1 small onion, finely chopped
- 250ml heavy cream
- 50g grated Parmesan cheese
- 2 tablespoons fresh parsley, chopped, for garnish (optional)

Instructions:

1. Cook the tagliatelle pasta according to the package instructions until al dente. Drain and set aside.

2. Heat the olive oil in a large pan or skillet over medium-high heat.

3. Season the chicken breast strips with salt and pepper. Add them to the pan and cook for about 5-6 minutes until they are cooked through and golden brown. Remove the chicken from the pan and set aside.

4. In the same pan, add the sliced mushrooms and cook for about 5 minutes until they start to soften and brown.

5. Add the minced garlic and chopped onion to the pan. Sauté for an additional 2-3 minutes until fragrant and the onion becomes translucent.

6. Reduce the heat to medium-low and pour in the heavy cream. Stir well to combine with the mushrooms, garlic, and onion.

7. Stir in the grated Parmesan cheese and cook for a few minutes until the sauce thickens slightly.

8. Return the cooked chicken strips to the pan and toss them in the creamy mushroom sauce to coat.

9. Add the cooked tagliatelle pasta to the pan and toss everything together until the pasta is well coated with the sauce.

10. Cook for an additional 2-3 minutes until the pasta is

heated through.

11. Remove the pan from the heat.

12. Serve the chicken and mushroom tagliatelle hot, garnished with fresh chopped parsley, if desired.

Veggie Pad Thai

Prep Time: 15 minutes / Cook time: 15 minutes
Serves: 4

Ingredients:

- 200g rice noodles
- 2 tablespoons vegetable oil
- 1 onion, thinly sliced
- 2 cloves garlic, minced
- 1 red bell pepper, thinly sliced
- 1 carrot, julienned
- 100g bean sprouts
- 100g tofu, diced
- 2 tablespoons soy sauce
- 2 tablespoons tamarind paste
- 1 tablespoon brown sugar
- 1 tablespoon lime juice
- 2 tablespoons crushed peanuts
- Fresh cilantro, chopped (for garnish)
- Lime wedges (for serving)

Instructions:

1. Cook the rice noodles according to the package instructions until they are al dente. Drain and set aside.

2. In a large skillet or wok, heat the vegetable oil over medium-high heat. Add the onion and garlic and sauté for 2-3 minutes until they become fragrant and slightly softened.

3. Add the red bell pepper, carrot, beansprouts, and tofu to the skillet. Stir-fry for 3-4 minutes until the vegetables are crisp-tender and the tofu is lightly browned.

4. In a small bowl, whisk together the soy sauce, tamarind paste, brown sugar, and lime juice until well combined.

5. Push the vegetables and tofu to one side of the skillet and pour the sauce mixture into the other side. Cook for 1 minute to heat the sauce.

6. Add the cooked rice noodles to the skillet and toss everything together until the noodles are evenly coated with the sauce and the vegetables are well distributed.

7. Cook for an additional 2-3 minutes, stirring constantly, until the noodles are heated through.

8. Remove from heat and sprinkle crushed peanuts over the top. Garnish with fresh cilantro.

9. Serve the Veggie Pad Thai hot, with lime wedges on the side for squeezing over the noodles.

Vegetarian Chickpea Curry

Prep Time: 10 minutes / Cook Time: 25 minutes
Serves: 4

Ingredients:

- 2 tablespoons vegetable oil
- 1 onion, finely chopped
- 3 cloves of garlic, minced
- 1-inch piece of ginger, grated
- 2 teaspoons ground cumin
- 2 teaspoons ground coriander
- 1 teaspoon ground turmeric
- 1 teaspoon chilli powder (adjust to taste)
- 400g canned chickpeas, drained and rinsed
- 400g canned diced tomatoes
- 200ml coconut milk
- 200ml vegetable broth
- Salt, to taste
- Fresh cilantro, chopped, for garnish (optional)

Instructions:

1. Heat the vegetable oil in a large pan or skillet over medium heat.
2. Add the chopped onion and cook for about 5-6 minutes until it becomes soft and translucent.
3. Add the minced garlic and grated ginger to the pan. Cook for an additional 1-2 minutes until fragrant.
4. In a small bowl, mix together the ground cumin, ground coriander, ground turmeric, and chilli powder.
5. Sprinkle the spice mixture over the onions, garlic, and ginger in the pan. Stir well to coat the ingredients.
6. Add the drained and rinsed chickpeas to the pan and stir to combine with the spices.
7. Pour in the canned diced tomatoes, coconut milk, and vegetable broth. Stir well to combine all the ingredients.
8. Season with salt to taste. Bring the mixture to a simmer.
9. Reduce the heat to low and let the curry simmer for about 15 minutes, stirring occasionally to prevent sticking.
10. After 15 minutes, the flavours will have melded together and the curry will have thickened slightly.
11. Remove the pan from the heat.
12. Serve the vegetarian chickpea curry hot, accompanied by steamed rice or naan bread.
13. Garnish with fresh chopped cilantro, if desired.

Roast Quail with Bacon and Sage

Prep Time: 15 minutes / Cook Time: 30 minutes
Serves: 4

Ingredients:

- 4 quail, cleaned and dressed
- 8 slices of bacon
- 12 fresh sage leaves
- Salt and pepper, to taste
- 2 tablespoons olive oil
- 1 tablespoon butter
- 250ml chicken broth

Instructions:

1. Preheat the air fryer oven to 200°C.
2. Season the quail with salt and pepper, both inside and outside.
3. Place 3 sage leaves inside each quail cavity.
4. Wrap each quail with 2 slices of bacon, securing them with toothpicks if needed.
5. Heat the olive oil and butter in a large air fryer ovenproof skillet or roasting pan over medium-high heat.
6. Add the quail to the pan, breast-side down, and sear them for about 2-3 minutes until the bacon starts to crisp.
7. Flip the quail and sear the other side for an additional 2-3 minutes.
8. Pour the chicken broth into the pan, around the quail.
9. Transfer the pan to the preheated air fryer oven and roast the quail for about 20-25 minutes, or until they are cooked through and the bacon is crispy.
10. Baste the quail with the pan juices halfway through cooking.
11. Once cooked, remove the pan from the air fryer oven and let the quail rest for a few minutes.
12. Transfer the quail to a serving platter.
13. Remove the toothpicks from the quail and discard them.
14. Serve the roast quail with bacon and sage hot, accompanied by roasted potatoes, vegetables, or a fresh salad.

Pan-Fried Sea Bass with Lemon Butter Sauce

Prep Time: 10 minutes / Cook Time: 10 minutes
Serves: 2

Ingredients:

- 2 sea bass fillets
- Salt and pepper, to taste
- 2 tablespoons all-purpose flour
- 2 tablespoons vegetable oil
- 2 tablespoons unsalted butter
- Juice of 1 lemon
- 2 tablespoons fresh parsley, chopped, for garnish (optional)
- Lemon wedges, for serving

Instructions:

1. Pat the sea bass fillets dry with paper towels. Season them with salt and pepper on both sides.
2. Place the all-purpose flour in a shallow dish or plate. Dredge the sea bass fillets in the flour, shaking off any excess.
3. Heat the vegetable oil in a large skillet over medium-

high heat.

4. Once the oil is hot, carefully place the sea bass fillets in the skillet, skin-side down. Cook for about 4-5 minutes until the skin becomes crispy and golden brown.

5. Flip the fillets using a spatula and cook for an additional 2-3 minutes on the other side until the fish is cooked through and flakes easily with a fork.

6. Remove the sea bass fillets from the skillet and transfer them to a serving platter. Keep them warm.

7. In the same skillet, reduce the heat to medium-low and add the unsalted butter. Allow it to melt and start to bubble.

8. Squeeze the lemon juice into the skillet, being careful of any splattering.

9. Cook the lemon butter sauce for about 1-2 minutes, stirring constantly, until it thickens slightly.

10. Remove the skillet from the heat.

11. Pour the lemon butter sauce over the sea bass fillets, ensuring they are evenly coated.

12. Garnish with fresh chopped parsley, if desired.

13. Serve the pan-fried sea bass with lemon butter sauce hot, accompanied by steamed vegetables or a side salad.

14. Serve with lemon wedges on the side for an extra burst of citrus flavour.

Spicy Coconut Curry with Prawns

Prep Time: 15 minutes / Cook Time: 20 minutes
Serves: 4

Ingredients:

- 500g prawns, peeled and deveined
- 2 tablespoons vegetable oil
- 1 onion, finely chopped
- 3 cloves of garlic, minced
- 1-inch piece of ginger, grated
- 2 tablespoons red curry paste
- 400ml coconut milk
- 200ml vegetable broth
- 1 red bell pepper, thinly sliced
- 1 small zucchini, diced
- 1 tablespoon fish sauce
- 1 tablespoon soy sauce
- 1 tablespoon brown sugar
- Juice of 1 lime
- Fresh cilantro, chopped, for garnish (optional)
- Cooked rice, for serving

Instructions:

1. In a large pan or skillet, heat the vegetable oil over medium heat.

2. Add the chopped onion and cook for about 5 minutes until it becomes soft and translucent.

3. Add the minced garlic and grated ginger to the pan. Cook for an additional 1-2 minutes until fragrant.

4. Stir in the red curry paste and cook for another minute to release its flavours.

5. Pour in the coconut milk and vegetable broth. Stir well to combine.

6. Add the sliced red bell pepper and diced zucchini to the pan. Stir to coat the vegetables with the curry sauce.

7. Simmer the curry mixture over medium heat for about 10 minutes, allowing the flavours to meld together and the vegetables to become tender.

8. Stir in the fish sauce, soy sauce, brown sugar, and lime juice. Mix well to combine.

9. Add the prawns to the pan and cook for about 3-5 minutes until they turn pink and are cooked through.

10. Once cooked, remove the pan from the heat.

11. Serve the spicy coconut curry with prawns hot, accompanied by steamed rice.

12. Garnish with fresh chopped cilantro, if desired, for added freshness and aroma.

Pan-Seared Duck Breast with Red Wine Sauce

Prep Time: 10 minutes / Cook Time: 20 minutes
Serves: 2

Ingredients:

- 2 duck breast fillets
- Salt and pepper, to taste
- 1 tablespoon vegetable oil
- 2 tablespoons unsalted butter
- 1 shallot, finely chopped
- 2 cloves of garlic, minced
- 200ml red wine
- 200ml chicken broth
- 1 tablespoon balsamic vinegar
- 1 tablespoon honey
- Fresh thyme sprigs, for garnish (optional)

Instructions:

1. Score the skin of the duck breast fillets with a sharp knife, making diagonal cuts about ½-inch apart. This helps render the fat and creates a crispy skin when cooked. Season the duck breasts generously with salt and pepper on both sides.

2. Heat the vegetable oil in a large skillet over medium-high heat.

3. Place the duck breasts in the skillet, skin-side down. Cook for about 6-8 minutes, or until the skin becomes crispy and golden brown. Use a spoon to pour off excess duck fat during cooking.

4. Flip the duck breasts using tongs and cook for an additional 2-3 minutes on the other side to achieve a medium-rare to medium doneness. Adjust the cooking time according to your preference.

5. Transfer the duck breasts to a cutting board and let them rest for a few minutes.

6. In the same skillet, reduce the heat to medium and melt the unsalted butter.

7. Add the chopped shallot and minced garlic to the

skillet. Sauté for about 2-3 minutes until the shallot becomes soft and translucent.

8. Pour in the red wine, chicken broth, balsamic vinegar, and honey. Stir well to combine.
9. Increase the heat to medium-high and bring the sauce to a simmer. Cook for about 8-10 minutes, stirring occasionally, until the sauce reduces and thickens slightly.
10. While the sauce is simmering, slice the rested duck breasts diagonally into thin slices.
11. Arrange the duck slices on serving plates.
12. Pour the red wine sauce over the duck slices, ensuring they are evenly coated.
13. Garnish with fresh thyme sprigs, if desired.
14. Serve the pan-seared duck breast with red wine sauce hot, accompanied by roasted potatoes, steamed vegetables, or a side salad.

Brussels Sprouts

Prep Time: 10 minutes / Cook time: 20 minutes
Serves: 4

Ingredients:

- 450g Brussels sprouts
- 30ml olive oil
- Salt and pepper to taste

Instructions:

1. Preheat the oven to 200°C.
2. Trim the ends of the Brussels sprouts and remove any outer leaves that are damaged or discoloured.
3. Cut the Brussels sprouts in half lengthwise.
4. Place the Brussels sprouts on a baking sheet and drizzle with olive oil. Toss to coat them evenly.
5. Season with salt and pepper to taste.
6. Roast in the preheated oven for about 20 minutes or until the Brussels sprouts are tender and lightly browned, stirring once halfway through.
7. Remove from the oven and serve hot.

Fried Green Beans

Prep Time: 15 minutes / Cook time: 15 minutes
Serves: 4

Ingredients:

- 225g green beans, ends trimmed
- 60g all-purpose flour
- 60g cornmeal
- 1 teaspoon paprika
- 1/2 teaspoon garlic powder
- 1/2 teaspoon salt
- 1/4 teaspoon black pepper
- Vegetable oil, for frying

Instructions:

1. In a shallow dish, combine the flour, cornmeal, paprika, garlic powder, salt, and black pepper.
2. Heat vegetable oil in a large skillet or deep fryer to

around 175°C.
3. Dip the green beans in the flour mixture, shaking off any excess.
4. Carefully add the coated green beans to the hot oil, in batches if necessary to avoid overcrowding the skillet.
5. Fry the green beans for about 3-4 minutes or until they become crispy and golden brown.
6. Use a slotted spoon or tongs to transfer the fried green beans to a paper towel-lined plate to drain excess oil.
7. Repeat the process with the remaining green beans.
8. Serve the fried green beans hot as a delicious side dish or snack.

Broccoli Tots

Prep Time: 15 minutes / Cook time: 20 minutes
Serves: 4

Ingredients:

- 400g broccoli florets
- 60g breadcrumbs
- 60g grated Parmesan cheese
- 1 large egg, beaten
- 1/2 teaspoon garlic powder
- 1/2 teaspoon onion powder
- Salt and pepper to taste

Instructions:

1. Preheat the oven to 200°C.
2. Steam the broccoli florets until tender, about 5-6 minutes. Drain and pat them dry using a clean kitchen towel or paper towels.
3. Chop the steamed broccoli finely or pulse it in a food processor until crumbly.
4. In a mixing bowl, combine the chopped broccoli, breadcrumbs, grated Parmesan cheese, beaten egg, garlic powder, onion powder, salt, and pepper. Mix well until all the ingredients are evenly incorporated.
5. Shape the mixture into small tots or cylindrical shapes using your hands, pressing them tightly to hold their form.
6. Place the tots on a baking sheet lined with parchment paper or greased with oil.
7. Bake in the preheated oven for about 18-20 minutes, or until the tots are golden brown and crispy.
8. Remove from the oven and let them cool slightly before serving. Serve hot as a tasty snack or side dish.

Parmesan Roasted Green Beans

Prep Time: 10 minutes / Cook time: 15 minutes
Serves: 4

Ingredients:

- 400g green beans, ends trimmed
- 30ml olive oil
- 30g grated Parmesan cheese
- 1/2 teaspoon garlic powder

- Salt and pepper to taste

Instructions:

1. Preheat the oven to 220°C.
2. In a mixing bowl, combine the green beans, olive oil, grated Parmesan cheese, garlic powder, salt, and pepper. Toss well to coat the green beans evenly with the mixture.
3. Spread the coated green beans in a single layer on a baking sheet lined with parchment paper.
4. Roast in the preheated oven for about 12-15 minutes, or until the green beans are tender and slightly crispy, stirring once halfway through.
5. Remove from the oven and serve immediately.

Fried Okra

Prep Time: 15 minutes / Cook time: 15 minutes
Serves: 4

Ingredients:

- 400g okra, sliced into rounds
- 60g cornmeal
- 60g all-purpose flour
- 1/2 teaspoon paprika
- 1/2 teaspoon garlic powder
- 1/2 teaspoon salt
- 1/4 teaspoon black pepper

Instructions:

1. In a shallow dish, combine the cornmeal, all-purpose flour, paprika, garlic powder, salt, and black pepper.
2. Heat the oven or deep fryer to around 175°C.
3. Dip the okra slices in the flour mixture, shaking off any excess.
4. Carefully add the coated okra slices to the hot oil, in batches if necessary to avoid overcrowding the skillet.
5. Fry the okra for about 3-4 minutes or until they become crispy and golden brown.
6. Use a slotted spoon or tongs to transfer the fried okra to a paper towel-lined plate to drain excess oil.
7. Repeat the process with the remaining okra slices.
8. Serve the fried okra hot as a delicious side dish or snack.

Garlic Mushrooms

Prep Time: 10 minutes / Cook time: 15 minutes
Serves: 4

Ingredients:

- 400g mushrooms, sliced
- 2 tablespoons butter
- 2 tablespoons olive oil
- 4 cloves garlic, minced
- 1 tablespoon chopped fresh parsley
- Salt and pepper to taste

Instructions:

1. Heat the butter and olive oil in a large skillet over medium heat until the butter is melted.
2. Add the minced garlic to the skillet and sauté for about 1 minute, until fragrant.
3. Add the sliced mushrooms to the skillet and cook for about 10-12 minutes, or until the mushrooms have softened and released their moisture.
4. Stir in the chopped parsley and season with salt and pepper to taste. Cook for an additional 2-3 minutes.
5. Remove from heat and serve the garlic mushrooms hot as a flavourful side dish or topping.

Kale Chips

Prep Time: 10 minutes / Cook time: 15 minutes
Serves: 4

Ingredients:

- 200g kale leaves, stems removed and torn into bite-sized pieces
- 1 tablespoon olive oil
- Salt and pepper to taste

Instructions:

1. Preheat the oven to 175°C.
2. In a large mixing bowl, combine the kale leaves, olive oil, salt, and pepper. Toss well to coat the kale leaves evenly with the oil and seasonings.
3. Spread the kale leaves in a single layer on a baking sheet lined with parchment paper.
4. Bake in the preheated oven for about 12-15 minutes, or until the kale leaves are crispy and lightly browned. Keep a close eye on them to prevent burning.
5. Remove from the oven and let them cool slightly before serving. The kale chips will become crispier as they cool down.
6. Serve the kale chips as a healthy and delicious snack.

Vegetable Tempura

Prep Time: 20 minutes / Cook time: 15 minutes
Serves: 4

Ingredients:

- 200g mixed vegetables (such as bell peppers, broccoli florets, carrot slices, and zucchini), cut into bite-sized pieces
- 100g all-purpose flour
- 2 tablespoons cornstarch
- 1/2 teaspoon baking powder
- 1/4 teaspoon salt
- 200ml ice-cold water
- Vegetable oil, for frying
- Dipping sauce of your choice (e.g., soy sauce, sweet chilli sauce)

Instructions:

1. In a mixing bowl, combine the all-purpose flour, cornstarch, baking powder, and salt.
2. Gradually pour in the ice-cold water while whisking

the mixture until you get a smooth batter.

3. Heat vegetable oil in a deep skillet or saucepan to around 180°C.
4. Dip the mixed vegetables into the batter, making sure they are coated evenly.
5. Carefully add the coated vegetables to the hot oil, in batches if necessary to avoid overcrowding the pan. Fry for about 2-3 minutes, or until the tempura turns golden brown and crispy.
6. Use a slotted spoon or tongs to transfer the fried vegetables to a paper towel-lined plate to drain excess oil.
7. Repeat the process with the remaining vegetables.
8. Serve the vegetable tempura hot with your preferred dipping sauce.

Stuffed Zucchini Boats

Recipe: Stuffed Zucchini Boats
Prep Time: 15 minutes / Cook time: 25 minutes
Serves: 4

Ingredients:

- 4 medium zucchini
- 200g ground meat (e.g., beef, chicken, or turkey)
- 1/2 onion, finely chopped
- 2 cloves garlic, minced
- 1/2 red bell pepper, diced
- 56g grated cheese (such as mozzarella or cheddar)
- 1 tablespoon olive oil
- 1 teaspoon dried herbs (e.g., oregano, basil, or thyme)
- Salt and pepper to taste

Instructions:

1. Preheat the oven to 200°C.
2. Cut the zucchini in half lengthwise, and use a spoon to scoop out the seeds and create a hollow centre in each zucchini half.
3. In a skillet, heat the olive oil over medium heat. Add the chopped onion, minced garlic, and diced red bell pepper. Sauté until the vegetables are softened.
4. Add the ground meat to the skillet and cook until browned. Season with dried herbs, salt, and pepper.
5. Fill each zucchini half with the ground meat mixture, pressing it gently into the hollowed center.
6. Place the stuffed zucchini boats on a baking sheet. Bake in the preheated oven for about 20-25 minutes, or until the zucchini is tender and the filling is cooked through.
7. Sprinkle grated cheese over the stuffed zucchini boats and return them to the oven for an additional 3-5 minutes, or until the cheese is melted and bubbly.
8. Remove from the oven and let them cool slightly before serving. Serve the stuffed zucchini boats as a flavourful main dish or side.

Garlic and Herb Roasted Carrots

Prep Time: 10 minutes / Cook time: 25 minutes
Serves: 4

Ingredients:

- 400g carrots, peeled and cut into sticks
- 2 tablespoons olive oil
- 3 cloves garlic, minced
- 1 teaspoon dried herbs (such as rosemary, thyme, or parsley)
- Salt and pepper to taste

Instructions:

1. Preheat the oven to 200°C.
2. In a mixing bowl, combine the carrot sticks, olive oil, minced garlic, dried herbs, salt, and pepper. Toss well to coat the carrots evenly with the oil and seasonings.
3. Spread the coated carrot sticks in a single layer on a baking sheet lined with parchment paper.
4. Roast in the preheated oven for about 20-25 minutes, or until the carrots are tender and caramelised, stirring once halfway through.
5. Remove from the oven and serve the garlic and herb roasted carrots hot as a flavourful side dish.

Stuffed Tomatoes

Prep Time: 15 minutes / Cook time: 20 minutes
Serves: 4

Ingredients:

- 4 large tomatoes
- 200g cooked rice
- 1/2 onion, finely chopped
- 2 cloves garlic, minced
- 50g grated cheese (such as mozzarella or cheddar)
- 2 tablespoons chopped fresh herbs (such as basil or parsley)
- Salt and pepper to taste
- Olive oil, for drizzling

Instructions:

1. Preheat the oven to 180°C.
2. Slice off the tops of the tomatoes and scoop out the seeds and pulp using a spoon, creating a hollow centre in each tomato.
3. In a mixing bowl, combine the cooked rice, finely chopped onion, minced garlic, grated cheese, chopped fresh herbs, salt, and pepper. Mix well until all the ingredients are evenly incorporated.
4. Fill each hollowed tomato with the rice mixture, pressing it gently into the tomato.
5. Place the stuffed tomatoes in a baking dish. Drizzle a little olive oil over the tops of the tomatoes.
6. Bake in the preheated oven for about 18-20 minutes, or until the tomatoes are softened and the filling is heated through.
7. Remove from the oven and let them cool slightly before serving. Serve the stuffed tomatoes as a delicious and colourful side dish or light meal.

Chapter 3 Fish and Seafood Recipes

Seafood Paella

Prep Time: 20 minutes / Cook time: 40 minutes
Serves: 4

Ingredients:

- 300g paella rice
- 500ml seafood stock
- 200g large shrimp, peeled and deveined
- 200g mussels, cleaned and debearded
- 200g squid, cleaned and sliced into rings
- 1 onion, diced
- 1 red bell pepper, diced
- 2 cloves garlic, minced
- 2 tomatoes, diced
- 100g frozen peas
- 1 teaspoon smoked paprika
- 1/2 teaspoon saffron threads
- Salt and pepper to taste
- 30ml olive oil
- Lemon wedges, for serving
- Fresh parsley, chopped, for garnish

Instructions:

1. In a small bowl, combine the saffron threads with 2 tablespoons of hot water and let it steep for 5 minutes.
2. Heat olive oil in a large paella pan or skillet over medium heat. Add the diced onion and red bell pepper, and sauté until they soften, about 5 minutes. Add the minced garlic and cook for an additional minute.
3. Add the diced tomatoes and cook for about 5 minutes, until they break down and release their juices.
4. Stir in the paella rice, smoked paprika, and saffron mixture. Season with salt and pepper to taste. Cook for 2 minutes, stirring to coat the rice with the spices.
5. Pour in the seafood stock and bring it to a simmer. Reduce the heat to low, cover the pan, and let it cook for about 15 minutes, or until the rice is almost tender.
6. Add the frozen peas, shrimp, mussels, and squid to the pan, pushing them into the rice. Cover the pan and cook for an additional 5-7 minutes, or until the seafood is cooked through and the mussels have opened.
7. Remove the pan from heat and let it rest, covered, for 5 minutes.
8. Garnish with freshly chopped parsley and serve the seafood paella hot, accompanied by lemon wedges for squeezing over the dish.

Baked Stuffed Plaice with Herbed Breadcrumbs

Prep Time: 15 minutes / Cook time: 25 minutes
Serves: 4

Ingredients:

- 4 plaice fillets
- 50g breadcrumbs
- 2 tablespoons fresh parsley, chopped
- 1 tablespoon fresh dill, chopped
- 1 tablespoon fresh chives, chopped
- 2 tablespoons butter, melted
- 1 lemon, zested
- Salt and pepper to taste
- Olive oil, for drizzling

Instructions:

1. Preheat the oven to 200°C.
2. In a bowl, combine the breadcrumbs, chopped fresh parsley, dill, chives, melted butter, lemon zest, salt, and pepper. Mix well until all the ingredients are evenly incorporated.
3. Place the plaice fillets on a baking sheet lined with parchment paper. Season the fillets with salt and pepper.
4. Divide the herbed breadcrumb mixture evenly among the plaice fillets, spreading it over the top of each fillet.
5. Drizzle a little olive oil over the breadcrumb topping.
6. Bake in the preheated oven for about 20-25 minutes, or until the fish is cooked through and the breadcrumbs are golden brown and crispy.
7. Remove from the oven and serve the baked stuffed plaice fillets hot, accompanied by your choice of sides such as steamed vegetables or a fresh salad. Garnish with additional fresh herbs, if desired. Enjoy the baked stuffed plaice with herbed breadcrumbs as a delicious and flavourful seafood dish.

Grilled Garlic and Herb King Prawns

Prep Time: 15 minutes / Cook time: 5 minutes
Serves: 4

Ingredients:

- 500g king prawns, peeled and deveined
- 3 cloves garlic, minced
- 2 tablespoons fresh parsley, chopped
- 2 tablespoons fresh dill, chopped
- 2 tablespoons olive oil
- 1 tablespoon lemon juice
- Salt and pepper to taste

Instructions:

1. In a bowl, combine the minced garlic, chopped fresh parsley, chopped fresh dill, olive oil, lemon juice, salt, and pepper. Mix well to create a marinade.
2. Add the king prawns to the marinade and toss to coat them evenly. Allow the prawns to marinate for about 10 minutes.

3. Preheat a grill or grill pan over medium-high heat.
4. Thread the marinated prawns onto skewers, leaving a little space between each prawn.
5. Grill the prawns for about 2-3 minutes per side, or until they turn pink and opaque. Be careful not to overcook them as they can become tough.
6. Once cooked, remove the prawns from the skewers and transfer them to a serving plate.

Cajun Blackened Salmon with Mango Salsa

Prep Time: 15 minutes / Cook time: 10 minutes
Serves: 4

Ingredients:
- 4 salmon fillets
- 2 tablespoons Cajun seasoning
- 1 tablespoon paprika
- 1 teaspoon garlic powder
- 1 teaspoon onion powder
- 1/2 teaspoon cayenne pepper (optional, for extra heat)
- Salt and pepper to taste
- 2 tablespoons olive oil

For the Mango Salsa:
- 1 ripe mango, peeled and diced
- 1/2 red bell pepper, diced
- 1/4 red onion, finely chopped
- 2 tablespoons fresh cilantro, chopped
- 1 tablespoon lime juice
- Salt to taste

Instructions:
1. In a small bowl, combine the Cajun seasoning, paprika, garlic powder, onion powder, cayenne pepper (if using), salt, and pepper. Mix well to create the blackening spice blend.
2. Pat the salmon fillets dry with a paper towel. Rub both sides of each fillet with the blackening spice blend, ensuring they are evenly coated.
3. Heat olive oil in a large skillet over medium-high heat.
4. Place the seasoned salmon fillets in the skillet, skin-side down. Cook for about 3-4 minutes per side, or until the salmon is cooked to your desired level of doneness. The salmon should be flaky and opaque.
5. While the salmon is cooking, prepare the mango salsa. In a bowl, combine the diced mango, diced red bell pepper, finely chopped red onion, chopped fresh cilantro, lime juice, and salt. Mix well to combine.
6. Once the salmon is cooked, remove it from the skillet and transfer to a serving plate.
7. Serve the Cajun blackened salmon hot, topped with the refreshing mango salsa. It pairs well with steamed rice, quinoa, or a side of roasted vegetables.

Thai-style Fish Cakes with Sweet chilli Sauce

Prep Time: 20 minutes / Cook time: 10 minutes
Serves: 4

Ingredients:
- 500g white fish fillets (such as cod or haddock), deboned and skinless
- 2 cloves garlic, minced
- 2 tablespoons Thai red curry paste
- 1 tablespoon fish sauce
- 1 tablespoon lime juice
- 2 tablespoons fresh cilantro, chopped
- 2 tablespoons green onions, finely sliced
- 1 egg
- 50g breadcrumbs
- Vegetable oil, for frying
- Sweet chilli sauce, for serving

Instructions:
1. In a food processor, combine the white fish fillets, minced garlic, Thai red curry paste, fish sauce, lime juice, chopped fresh cilantro, and sliced green onions. Pulse until the ingredients are well combined and form a smooth mixture.
2. Transfer the fish mixture to a bowl. Add the egg and breadcrumbs. Mix well until all the ingredients are evenly incorporated.
3. Shape the mixture into small patties or fish cakes, about 5-7cm in diameter.
4. Heat vegetable oil in a frying pan over medium heat. Fry the fish cakes in batches until golden brown and cooked through, about 3-4 minutes per side.
5. Once cooked, remove the fish cakes from the pan and drain them on a paper towel to remove any excess oil.
6. Serve the Thai-style fish cakes hot, accompanied by sweet chilli sauce for dipping.

Creamy Garlic Butter Mussels

Prep Time: 15 minutes / Cook time: 10 minutes
Serves: 4

Ingredients:
- 1000g fresh mussels, cleaned and debearded
- 30g butter
- 4 cloves garlic, minced
- 120ml white wine
- 120ml heavy cream
- 2 tablespoons fresh parsley, chopped
- Salt and pepper to taste
- Fresh lemon wedges, for serving
- Crusty bread, for serving

Instructions:
1. Heat butter in a large pot or skillet over medium heat. Add the minced garlic and sauté for about 1 minute until fragrant.
2. Add the cleaned and debearded mussels to the pot. Pour in the white wine and cover the pot with a lid. Steam the mussels for about 4-5 minutes, or until they open up. Discard any mussels that remain closed after cooking.
3. Using a slotted spoon, transfer the cooked mussels to a

serving bowl, leaving the cooking liquid in the pot.

4. Pour the heavy cream into the pot with the cooking liquid. Stir well and let it simmer for a few minutes until the sauce slightly thickens.

5. Season the sauce with salt, pepper, and chopped fresh parsley. Stir to combine.

6. Pour the creamy garlic butter sauce over the cooked mussels in the serving bowl.

7. Serve the creamy garlic butter mussels hot, accompanied by fresh lemon wedges and crusty bread. They make a delightful seafood dish that can be enjoyed as an appetiser or as a main course.

Dover Sole with Brown Butter and Capers

Prep Time: 10 minutes / Cook time: 10 minutes
Serves: 4

Ingredients:

- 4 Dover sole fillets
- Salt and pepper to taste
- 60g unsalted butter
- 1 tablespoon fresh lemon juice
- 2 tablespoons capers, drained
- Fresh parsley, chopped for garnish
- Lemon wedges, for serving

Instructions:

1. Season the Dover sole fillets with salt and pepper on both sides.

2. In a large skillet, melt the butter over medium heat. Continue cooking until the butter starts to brown and has a nutty aroma, about 3-4 minutes. Be careful not to burn the butter.

3. Place the seasoned sole fillets in the skillet and cook for about 2-3 minutes on each side, or until they turn golden brown and are cooked through.

4. Remove the cooked sole fillets from the skillet and transfer them to a serving plate.

5. Pour the lemon juice into the skillet and add the capers. Cook for an additional 1-2 minutes, stirring gently.

6. Pour the brown butter and caper sauce over the cooked Dover sole fillets.

7. Garnish with fresh chopped parsley and serve the Dover sole hot, accompanied by lemon wedges. It pairs well with steamed vegetables or a side of roasted potatoes.

Creamy Garlic Prawns

Prep Time: 10 minutes / Cook time: 10 minutes
Serves: 4

Ingredients:

- 500g prawns, peeled and deveined
- 3 cloves garlic, minced
- 2 tablespoons butter
- 120ml heavy cream
- 2 tablespoons fresh parsley, chopped
- Salt and pepper to taste
- Lemon wedges, for serving

Instructions:

1. In a large skillet, melt the butter over medium heat. Add the minced garlic and sauté for about 1 minute until fragrant.

2. Add the prawns to the skillet and cook for about 3-4 minutes, or until they turn pink and opaque.

3. Reduce the heat to low and pour the heavy cream into the skillet. Stir well to combine the cream with the garlic and butter.

4. Simmer the prawns in the creamy garlic sauce for an additional 2-3 minutes, or until the sauce thickens slightly. Season with salt and pepper to taste.

5. Remove the skillet from the heat and garnish the creamy garlic prawns with fresh chopped parsley.

6. Serve the creamy garlic prawns hot, accompanied by lemon wedges.

Sea Bass with Salsa Verde

Prep Time: 15 minutes / Cook time: 15 minutes
Serves: 4 servings

Ingredients:

- 4 sea bass fillets
- Salt and pepper to taste
- Olive oil for drizzling

For the Salsa Verde:

- 1 bunch fresh parsley, leaves picked and chopped
- 1 small bunch fresh basil, leaves picked and chopped
- 2 tablespoons capers, drained and chopped
- 2 anchovy fillets, finely chopped
- 2 cloves garlic, minced
- 1 tablespoon lemon juice
- 120ml extra-virgin olive oil
- Salt and pepper to taste

Instructions:

1. Preheat the oven to 200°C.

2. Season the sea bass fillets with salt and pepper on both sides.

3. Drizzle some olive oil over the sea bass fillets and rub it gently to coat them.

4. Place the seasoned sea bass fillets on a baking sheet lined with parchment paper.

5. In a bowl, combine the chopped parsley, chopped basil, chopped capers, finely chopped anchovy fillets, minced garlic, lemon juice, and extra-virgin olive oil. Mix well to create the salsa verde. Season with salt and pepper to taste.

6. Spread a generous amount of the salsa verde over the top of each sea bass fillet.

7. Bake the sea bass fillets in the preheated oven for about 12-15 minutes, or until they are cooked through

and flake easily with a fork.

8. Once cooked, remove the sea bass fillets from the oven and let them rest for a few minutes.

9. Serve the sea bass with salsa verde hot, accompanied by your choice of side dishes like roasted potatoes or steamed vegetables.

Baked Cod with Herbed Breadcrumbs

Prep Time: 10 minutes / Cook time: 15 minutes
Serves: 4 servings

Ingredients:

- 4 cod fillets
- Salt and pepper to taste
- 60g breadcrumbs
- 2 tablespoons fresh parsley, chopped
- 1 tablespoon fresh thyme leaves
- 2 cloves garlic, minced
- Zest of 1 lemon
- 2 tablespoons melted butter

Instructions:

1. Preheat the oven to 200°C.
2. Season the cod fillets with salt and pepper on both sides.
3. In a bowl, combine the breadcrumbs, chopped parsley, thyme leaves, minced garlic, and lemon zest. Mix well to incorporate all the ingredients.
4. Place the seasoned cod fillets on a baking sheet lined with parchment paper.
5. Press the breadcrumb mixture onto the top of each cod fillet, ensuring it adheres well.
6. Drizzle the melted butter over the breadcrumb topping.
7. Bake the cod fillets in the preheated oven for about 12-15 minutes, or until they are cooked through and the breadcrumbs turn golden brown.
8. Once cooked, remove the cod fillets from the oven and let them rest for a few minutes.
9. Serve the baked cod with herbed breadcrumbs hot, accompanied by your choice of side dishes like roasted vegetables or a fresh salad.

Fish Pie with Cheesy Mashed Potatoes

Prep Time: 30 minutes/ Cook time: 45 minutes
Serves: 4-6 servings

Ingredients:

- 500g white fish fillets, such as cod or haddock, cut into chunks
- 200g smoked haddock fillets, skin removed, cut into chunks
- 200g peeled raw prawns
- 1 leek, thinly sliced
- 1 carrot, diced
- 200ml fish stock
- 200ml whole milk
- 2 tablespoons all-purpose flour
- 2 tablespoons butter
- 2 tablespoons chopped fresh parsley
- Salt and pepper to taste

For the Cheesy Mashed Potatoes:
- 800g potatoes, peeled and cut into chunks
- 100ml milk
- 50g butter
- 100g grated cheddar cheese
- Salt and pepper to taste

Instructions:

1. Preheat the oven to 200°C.
2. In a large saucepan, melt the butter over medium heat. Add the leek and carrot and cook for about 5 minutes until softened.
3. Stir in the flour and cook for another minute.
4. Gradually add the fish stock and milk, stirring constantly to avoid lumps. Cook for a few minutes until the sauce thickens.
5. Add the white fish fillets, smoked haddock, and prawns to the sauce. Stir gently to combine. Cook for about 5 minutes until the fish is cooked through and the prawns turn pink.
6. Stir in the chopped parsley and season with salt and pepper to taste.
7. Transfer the fish mixture to a baking dish.
8. To prepare the cheesy mashed potatoes, cook the potatoes in a large pot of boiling water until tender. Drain well.
9. In the same pot, heat the milk and butter over low heat until the butter melts. Remove from heat.
10. Add the cooked potatoes back to the pot and mash them until smooth. Stir in the grated cheddar cheese until melted and well combined. Season with salt and pepper.
11. Spread the cheesy mashed potatoes over the fish mixture in the baking dish, ensuring it covers the filling completely.
12. Place the baking dish in the preheated oven and bake for about 25-30 minutes until the top is golden and bubbling.
13. Remove from the oven and let it cool for a few minutes before serving. Serve the fish pie with cheesy mashed potatoes hot.

Grilled Prawns with Garlic and Lime

Prep Time: 15 minutes / Cook time: 6 minutes
Serves: 4 servings

Ingredients:

- 500g large prawns, peeled and deveined
- 3 cloves garlic, minced
- Zest and juice of 1 lime
- 2 tablespoons olive oil
- Salt and pepper to taste
- Fresh cilantro or parsley, chopped for garnish
- Lime wedges, for serving

Instructions:

1. In a bowl, combine the minced garlic, lime zest, lime juice, olive oil, salt, and pepper. Mix well to create a marinade.
2. Add the prawns to the marinade and toss to coat them evenly. Allow them to marinate for about 15-20 minutes.
3. Preheat the grill to medium-high heat.
4. Thread the marinated prawns onto skewers, leaving a small space between each prawn.
5. Grill the prawns for about 2-3 minutes per side, or until they turn pink and opaque.
6. Remove the prawn skewers from the grill and transfer them to a serving platter.
7. Garnish with fresh chopped cilantro or parsley.
8. Serve the grilled prawns with garlic and lime hot, accompanied by lime

Crispy Battered Calamari Rings

Prep Time: 15 minutes / Cook time: 15 minutes
Serves: 4 servings

Ingredients:

- 500g calamari rings
- 150g all-purpose flour
- 1 teaspoon paprika
- 1/2 teaspoon garlic powder
- 1/2 teaspoon salt
- 1/4 teaspoon black pepper
- 240ml cold sparkling water
- Vegetable oil, for frying
- Lemon wedges, for serving

Instructions:

1. In a mixing bowl, combine the flour, paprika, garlic powder, salt, and black pepper. Mix well.
2. Gradually add the sparkling water to the flour mixture, whisking until a smooth batter forms.
3. Heat vegetable oil in a deep frying pan or pot over medium-high heat or preheat an air fryer until it reaches 180°C.
4. Dip the calamari rings into the batter, coating them evenly.
5. Carefully place the battered calamari rings into the hot oil, a few at a time, and fry for about 2-3 minutes until they turn golden brown and crispy.
6. Use a slotted spoon to remove the cooked calamari rings from the oil and transfer them to a plate lined with paper towels to drain excess oil.
7. Repeat the frying process with the remaining calamari rings.
8. Serve the crispy battered calamari rings hot, accompanied by lemon wedges for squeezing over the top.

Oven-Roasted Trout with Herbs

Prep Time: 10 minutes / Cook time: 20 minutes
Serves: 2 servings

Ingredients:

- 2 whole trout, cleaned and gutted

- Salt and pepper to taste
- 2 tablespoons olive oil
- 2 cloves garlic, minced
- 1 tablespoon fresh lemon juice
- 1 tablespoon chopped fresh herbs (such as parsley, thyme, or dill)

Instructions:

1. Preheat the oven to 200°C.
2. Season the trout inside and out with salt and pepper.
3. In a small bowl, combine the olive oil, minced garlic, lemon juice, and chopped fresh herbs.
4. Rub the herb mixture all over the trout, making sure to coat both sides.
5. Place the seasoned trout on a baking sheet lined with parchment paper.
6. Roast the trout in the preheated oven for about 15-20 minutes until the flesh is opaque and flakes easily with a fork.
7. Once cooked, remove the trout from the oven and let it rest for a few minutes before serving.
8. Serve the oven-roasted trout hot, accompanied by your choice of side dishes like roasted potatoes or steamed vegetables.

Steamed Mussels in White Wine and Garlic Sauce

Prep Time: 10 minutes / Cook time: 10 minutes
Serves: 4 servings

Ingredients:

- 2000g fresh mussels, cleaned and debearded
- 30ml olive oil
- 4 cloves garlic, minced
- 240ml dry white wine
- 15g chopped fresh parsley
- Salt and pepper to taste
- Crusty bread, for serving

Instructions:

1. In a large pot or Dutch oven, heat the olive oil over medium heat. Add the minced garlic and sauté for about 1 minute until fragrant.
2. Add the white wine to the pot and bring it to a simmer.
3. Add the cleaned mussels to the pot and cover with a lid. Steam the mussels for about 5-7 minutes or until they open up. Discard any mussels that remain closed.
4. Remove the pot from the heat and sprinkle the steamed mussels with chopped fresh parsley. Season with salt and pepper to taste.
5. Serve the steamed mussels in bowls, ladling some of the white wine and garlic sauce over the top. Serve with crusty bread on the side for dipping.

Grilled Tuna Steak with Chimichurri Sauce

Prep Time: 15 minutes / Cook time: 6-8 minutes
Serves: 2 servings

Ingredients:

- 2 tuna steaks

- 30ml olive oil
- Salt and pepper to taste

For the Chimichurri Sauce:
- 60ml fresh parsley, chopped
- 15ml fresh cilantro, chopped
- 2 cloves garlic, minced
- 30ml red wine vinegar
- 60ml extra-virgin olive oil
- 1/4 teaspoon red pepper flakes
- Salt and pepper to taste

Instructions:

1. Preheat the grill to medium-high heat.
2. Rub the tuna steaks with olive oil and season with salt and pepper.
3. In a small bowl, combine the chopped parsley, cilantro, minced garlic, red wine vinegar, extra-virgin olive oil, red pepper flakes, salt, and pepper. Mix well to make the chimichurri sauce.
4. Grill the tuna steaks for about 3-4 minutes per side for medium-rare, or adjust the cooking time according to your desired doneness.
5. Remove the tuna steaks from the grill and let them rest for a few minutes.
6. Serve the grilled tuna steaks with a generous drizzle of chimichurri sauce on top.

Grilled Swordfish with Tomato and Olive Salsa

Prep Time: 15 minutes/ Cook time: 10 minutes
Serves: 4 servings

Ingredients:

- 4 swordfish steaks (about 150g each)
- 30ml olive oil
- Salt and pepper to taste

For the Tomato and Olive Salsa:
- 200g cherry tomatoes, halved
- 60g pitted black olives, sliced
- 15ml fresh lemon juice
- 15ml extra-virgin olive oil
- 2 tablespoons chopped fresh parsley
- Salt and pepper to taste

Instructions:

1. Preheat the grill to medium-high heat.
2. Brush the swordfish steaks with olive oil and season with salt and pepper.
3. Place the swordfish steaks on the grill and cook for about 4-5 minutes per side, or until cooked through. The internal temperature should reach 63°C.
4. While the swordfish is grilling, prepare the tomato and olive salsa. In a bowl, combine the cherry tomatoes, black olives, lemon juice, extra-virgin olive oil, chopped parsley, salt, and pepper. Mix well.
5. Remove the grilled swordfish steaks from the grill and let them rest for a few minutes.
6. Serve the grilled swordfish steaks with a generous

spoonful of tomato and olive salsa on top.

Fish Tacos with Chipotle Lime Sauce

Prep Time: 20 minutes / Cook time: 10 minutes
Serves: 4 servings

Ingredients:

- 500g white fish fillets (such as cod or tilapia)
- 30ml olive oil
- 10ml fresh lime juice
- 2 cloves garlic, minced
- 10g chipotle chilli powder
- 8 small tortillas

For the Chipotle Lime Sauce:
- 120ml mayonnaise
- 15ml fresh lime juice
- 5g chipotle chilli powder
- Salt to taste

For Serving:
- Shredded lettuce
- Sliced avocado
- Chopped fresh cilantro
- Lime wedges

Instructions:

1. Preheat the grill or grill pan over medium-high heat.
2. In a small bowl, whisk together the olive oil, lime juice, minced garlic, and chipotle chilli powder.
3. Brush the fish fillets with the marinade mixture, coating them evenly.
4. Grill the fish fillets for about 3-4 minutes per side, or until cooked through and flaky.
5. While the fish is grilling, prepare the chipotle lime sauce. In a bowl, combine the mayonnaise, lime juice, chipotle chilli powder, and salt. Stir until well combined.
6. Warm the tortillas on the grill or in a dry skillet over medium heat.
7. To assemble the fish tacos, place a grilled fish fillet on each warmed tortilla. Top with shredded lettuce, sliced avocado, chopped cilantro, and a drizzle of chipotle lime sauce. Squeeze fresh lime juice over the top.
8. Serve the fish tacos immediately, and enjoy!

Crab Cakes with Remoulade Sauce

Prep Time: 20 minutes / Cook time: 10 minutes
Serves: 4 servings

Ingredients:

- 450g lump crab meat
- 60g breadcrumbs
- 2 tablespoons mayonnaise
- 1 tablespoon Dijon mustard
- 1 tablespoon Worcestershire sauce
- 1 tablespoon chopped fresh parsley
- 1 tablespoon chopped fresh chives
- 1/2 teaspoon Old Bay seasoning
- Salt and pepper to taste

- 2 tablespoons olive oil

For the Remoulade Sauce:
- 120ml mayonnaise
- 1 tablespoon Dijon mustard
- 1 tablespoon chopped fresh parsley
- 1 tablespoon chopped fresh chives
- 1 tablespoon capers, drained and chopped
- 1 tablespoon pickle relish
- 1 tablespoon fresh lemon juice
- Salt and pepper to taste

Instructions:

1. In a large bowl, gently combine the lump crab meat, breadcrumbs, mayonnaise, Dijon mustard, Worcestershire sauce, chopped parsley, chopped chives, Old Bay seasoning, salt, and pepper. Be careful not to overmix.
2. Form the mixture into crab cakes of desired size and thickness.
3. Heat the olive oil in a skillet over medium-high heat. Cook the crab cakes for about 3-4 minutes per side until golden brown and crispy.
4. While the crab cakes are cooking, prepare the remoulade sauce. In a small bowl, whisk together the mayonnaise, Dijon mustard, chopped parsley, chopped chives, capers, pickle relish, fresh lemon juice, salt, and pepper.
5. Serve the crab cakes hot, accompanied by the remoulade sauce for dipping.

Teriyaki Glazed Salmon

Prep Time: 10 minutes / Cook time: 12 minutes
Serves: 4 servings

Ingredients:
- 4 salmon fillets (about 150g each)
- 60ml soy sauce
- 60ml mirin
- 30ml honey
- 15ml rice vinegar
- 2 cloves garlic, minced
- 1 teaspoon grated fresh ginger
- 1 tablespoon cornstarch
- 1 tablespoon water
- Sesame seeds, for garnish
- Sliced green onions, for garnish

Instructions:

1. Preheat the oven to 200°C.
2. In a small saucepan, combine the soy sauce, mirin, honey, rice vinegar, minced garlic, and grated ginger. Bring the mixture to a simmer over medium heat and cook for about 2 minutes until the sauce slightly thickens.
3. In a separate bowl, whisk together the cornstarch and water to make a slurry. Add the slurry to the saucepan and cook for an additional 1-2 minutes until the sauce thickens to a glaze consistency. Remove from heat.

4. Place the salmon fillets on a baking sheet lined with parchment paper. Brush the teriyaki glaze generously over the salmon.
5. Bake the salmon in the preheated oven for about 10 minutes or until cooked through and flaky.
6. Remove the salmon from the oven and garnish with sesame seeds and sliced green onions.
7. Serve the teriyaki glazed salmon hot with steamed rice and vegetables, if desired.

Scallops with Pea Puree

Prep Time: 10 minutes / Cook time: 10 minutes
Serves: 4 servings

Ingredients:
- 12 large scallops
- Salt and pepper to taste
- 2 tablespoons olive oil
- 250g frozen peas, thawed
- 1 tablespoon fresh mint leaves, chopped
- 1 tablespoon fresh lemon juice
- Zest of 1 lemon
- 1 clove garlic, minced
- 30g butter
- Microgreens, for garnish (optional)

Instructions:

1. Pat dry the scallops with paper towels and season them with salt and pepper.
2. Heat 1 tablespoon of olive oil in a large skillet over medium-high heat. Add the scallops to the skillet and cook for about 2-3 minutes per side until golden brown and cooked through. Remove the scallops from the skillet and set them aside.
3. In a food processor, combine the thawed peas, chopped mint leaves, lemon juice, lemon zest, minced garlic, butter, salt, and pepper. Blend until smooth and creamy.
4. Heat the remaining 1 tablespoon of olive oil in the skillet over medium heat. Add the pea puree to the skillet and cook for about 2 minutes until heated through.
5. To serve, spoon the pea puree onto plates and arrange the cooked scallops on top. Garnish with microgreens if desired.

Fish and Spinach Curry

Prep Time: 15 minutes / Cook time: 25 minutes
Serves: 4 servings

Ingredients:
- 500g white fish fillets (such as cod or haddock), cut into bite-sized pieces
- 1 tablespoon vegetable oil
- 1 onion, finely chopped
- 2 cloves garlic, minced
- 1 tablespoon grated fresh ginger
- 2 teaspoons curry powder

- 1 teaspoon ground cumin
- 1 teaspoon ground coriander
- 1/2 teaspoon turmeric
- 1/4 teaspoon cayenne pepper (optional)
- 400ml coconut milk
- 200ml vegetable or fish broth
- 200g baby spinach leaves
- Salt and pepper to taste
- Fresh cilantro, for garnish
- Cooked rice, for serving

Instructions:

1. In a large skillet or saucepan, heat the vegetable oil over medium heat. Add the chopped onion and cook until softened and translucent, about 5 minutes.
2. Add the minced garlic and grated ginger to the skillet and cook for an additional 1 minute until fragrant.
3. Stir in the curry powder, cumin, coriander, turmeric, and cayenne pepper (if using) and cook for another 1 minute to toast the spices.
4. Pour in the coconut milk and vegetable or fish broth. Bring the mixture to a simmer and let it cook for about 10 minutes to allow the flavours to meld together.
5. Add the fish pieces to the skillet and gently stir to coat them with the sauce. Cook for about 5 minutes or until the fish is cooked through and flakes easily.
6. Stir in the baby spinach leaves and cook for another 2 minutes until wilted. Season with salt and pepper to taste.
7. Garnish the fish and spinach curry with fresh cilantro.
8. Serve the curry hot over cooked rice.

Spicy Cajun Baked Tilapia

Prep Time: 10 minutes / Cook time: 15 minutes
Serves: 4 servings

Ingredients:

- 4 tilapia fillets
- 2 tablespoons Cajun seasoning
- 1 teaspoon paprika
- 1/2 teaspoon garlic powder
- 1/2 teaspoon onion powder
- 1/4 teaspoon cayenne pepper (adjust according to spice preference)
- Salt and pepper to taste
- 2 tablespoons olive oil
- Lemon wedges, for serving
- Fresh parsley, chopped, for garnish

Instructions:

1. Preheat your oven to 200°C.
2. In a small bowl, combine the Cajun seasoning, paprika, garlic powder, onion powder, cayenne pepper, salt, and pepper.
3. Pat dry the tilapia fillets with paper towels. Rub both sides of each fillet with the Cajun spice mixture, ensuring they are evenly coated.

4. Heat the olive oil in an oven-safe skillet over medium-high heat. Once hot, add the seasoned tilapia fillets to the skillet and cook for about 2 minutes per side to sear them.
5. Transfer the skillet with the tilapia to the preheated oven and bake for about 10-12 minutes or until the fish is cooked through and flakes easily with a fork.
6. Remove the skillet from the oven and let the fish rest for a few minutes.
7. Serve the spicy Cajun baked tilapia hot, garnished with fresh parsley and accompanied by lemon wedges for squeezing over the fish.

Air Fryer Stuffed Chicken Breast with Spinach and Feta

Prep Time: 15 minutes / Cook time: 18-20 minutes
Serves: 4 servings

Ingredients:

- 4 boneless, skinless chicken breasts (approx. 120 g each)
- 100 g fresh spinach leaves, chopped
- 100 g crumbled feta cheese
- 1 clove garlic, minced
- 2 tbsp olive oil
- Salt and pepper, to taste
- 1 lemon, zested and juiced
- 2 tbsp all-purpose flour
- 2 tbsp Panko breadcrumbs
- 1 egg, beaten

Instructions:

1. Preheat the air fryer to 200°C.
2. In a bowl, mix together the chopped spinach, feta cheese, garlic, 1 tablespoon of the olive oil, salt, pepper, and lemon zest.
3. Use a sharp knife to make a pocket in the side of each chicken breast. Spoon the spinach mixture into each pocket, and secure with toothpicks.
4. In a shallow dish, mix together the flour, salt, pepper, and lemon juice.
5. In another shallow dish, place the beaten egg.
6. In a third shallow dish, place the Panko breadcrumbs.
7. Dip each chicken breast into the flour mixture, then the egg mixture, and finally the Panko mixture, making sure it is well coated.
8. Place the chicken breasts in a single layer in the air fryer basket.
9. Brush the remaining olive oil over the chicken.
10. Cook the chicken for 18-20 minutes, turning it halfway through cooking, until the internal temperature reaches 165°F (74°C) and the chicken is crispy and golden brown.
11. Serve the chicken with a side of the honey mustard dip. Enjoy!

Chapter 4 Poultry and Meat Recipes

Chicken Pot Pie

Prep Time: 20 minutes / Cook time: 40 minutes
Serves: 6 servings

Ingredients:

- 500g boneless, skinless chicken breasts, cubed
- 2 tablespoons olive oil
- 1 onion, diced
- 2 carrots, diced
- 2 celery stalks, diced
- 200g frozen peas
- 4 tablespoons butter
- 4 tablespoons all-purpose flour
- 480ml chicken broth
- 240ml milk
- Salt and pepper to taste
- 1 sheet of puff pastry, thawed
- 1 egg, beaten (for egg wash)

Instructions:

1. Preheat your oven to 200°C.
2. In a large skillet, heat the olive oil over medium-high heat. Add the cubed chicken and cook until browned and cooked through. Remove the chicken from the skillet and set aside.
3. In the same skillet, melt the butter over medium heat. Add the diced onion, carrots, and celery, and cook until the vegetables are tender, about 5 minutes.
4. Stir in the all-purpose flour and cook for 1-2 minutes until well combined.
5. Gradually whisk in the chicken broth and milk, making sure to eliminate any lumps. Cook the mixture until it thickens and comes to a simmer.
6. Add the cooked chicken and frozen peas to the skillet. Season with salt and pepper to taste. Stir to combine everything evenly.
7. Transfer the chicken mixture to a baking dish.
8. Roll out the puff pastry sheet to fit the size of your baking dish. Place the pastry on top of the filling, pressing the edges to seal.
9. Brush the pastry with the beaten egg to create a golden crust.
10. Cut a few slits on top of the pastry to allow steam to escape.
11. Bake the chicken pot pie in the preheated oven for about 30 minutes or until the pastry is golden brown and the filling is bubbling.
12. Remove from the oven and let it cool for a few minutes before serving.

Chicken Biryani

Prep Time: 20 minutes / Cook time: 40 minutes
Serves: 4-6 servings

Ingredients:

- 500g chicken thighs, bone-in, skinless, cut into pieces
- 400g basmati rice, rinsed and soaked for 30 minutes
- 2 onions, thinly sliced
- 2 tomatoes, chopped
- 4 cloves garlic, minced
- 1-inch piece of ginger, grated
- 2 green chillies, slit lengthwise (adjust according to spice preference)
- 1 teaspoon turmeric powder
- 1 teaspoon red chilli powder
- 1 teaspoon cumin powder
- 1 teaspoon coriander powder
- 1 teaspoon garam masala
- 120g plain yoghourt
- 15g chopped fresh cilantro
- 10g chopped fresh mint leaves
- 960g chicken broth
- 4 tablespoons ghee (clarified butter) or vegetable oil
- Salt to taste

Instructions:

1. In a large skillet or pot, heat the ghee or vegetable oil over medium heat. Add the sliced onions and cook until they turn golden brown and caramelised. Remove half of the onions and set them aside for garnishing.
2. To the remaining onions in the skillet, add the minced garlic, grated ginger, and green chillies. Sauté for 1-2 minutes until fragrant.
3. Add the chicken pieces to the skillet and cook until they are browned on all sides.
4. Stir in the chopped tomatoes, turmeric powder, red chilli powder, cumin powder, coriander powder, and salt. Cook for 2-3 minutes until the tomatoes soften.
5. Add the plain yoghourt, chopped cilantro, and chopped mint leaves. Mix well to coat the chicken with the spices.
6. Drain the soaked basmati rice and add it to the skillet. Stir gently to combine everything.
7. Pour in the chicken broth and bring the mixture to a boil. Once boiling, reduce the heat to low, cover the skillet, and let it simmer for about 20-25 minutes or until the rice is cooked and the chicken is tender.
8. Once cooked, remove from heat and let it rest for a few minutes.

9. Fluff the biryani gently with a fork and garnish with the reserved caramelised onions.
10. Serve the flavourful chicken biryani hot with raita (yoghourt sauce) or a side salad.

Lamb Moussaka

Recipe: Lamb Moussaka
Prep Time: 30 minutes / Cook time: 50 minutes
Serves: 6 servings

Ingredients:

- 500g ground lamb
- 2 large eggplants
- 2 tablespoons olive oil
- 1 onion, finely chopped
- 3 cloves garlic, minced
- 400g canned diced tomatoes
- 2 tablespoons tomato paste
- 1 teaspoon dried oregano
- 1 teaspoon dried thyme
- 1/2 teaspoon ground cinnamon
- Salt and pepper to taste
- 80g grated Parmesan cheese
- 240g béchamel sauce

Instructions:

1. Preheat your oven to 180°C.
2. Slice the eggplants into 1/4-inch thick rounds. Place them on a baking sheet, drizzle with olive oil, and season with salt and pepper. Roast in the preheated oven for 20-25 minutes or until tender. Set aside.
3. In a large skillet, heat olive oil over medium heat. Add the chopped onion and minced garlic, and sauté until they become soft and translucent.
4. Add the ground lamb to the skillet and cook until browned. Break up any large chunks with a spoon.
5. Stir in the diced tomatoes, tomato paste, dried oregano, dried thyme, ground cinnamon, salt, and pepper. Simmer the mixture for about 15 minutes to allow the flavours to meld.
6. Prepare a baking dish and layer half of the roasted eggplant slices at the bottom.
7. Spoon the lamb mixture evenly over the eggplant layer.
8. Add another layer of the remaining eggplant slices on top of the lamb mixture.
9. Pour the béchamel sauce over the eggplant layer, spreading it evenly.
10. Sprinkle the grated Parmesan cheese over the top.
11. Bake the moussaka in the preheated oven for 35-40 minutes or until the top is golden brown and bubbly.
12. Remove from the oven and let it rest for a few minutes before serving.

Lamb Kofta Kebabs

Prep Time: 20 minutes / Cook time: 15 minutes
Serves: 4 servings

Ingredients:

- 500g ground lamb
- 1 onion, finely chopped
- 3 cloves garlic, minced
- 2 tablespoons chopped fresh parsley
- 1 tablespoon chopped fresh mint leaves
- 1 teaspoon ground cumin
- 1 teaspoon ground coriander
- 1/2 teaspoon ground paprika
- 1/2 teaspoon ground cinnamon
- Salt and pepper to taste
- 4-6 wooden skewers, soaked in water

Instructions:

1. In a large mixing bowl, combine the ground lamb, chopped onion, minced garlic, chopped parsley, chopped mint leaves, ground cumin, ground coriander, ground paprika, ground cinnamon, salt, and pepper. Mix well until all the ingredients are evenly incorporated.
2. Divide the lamb mixture into equal portions and shape them into oblong kebab shapes around the soaked wooden skewers.
3. Preheat your grill or grill pan over medium-high heat.
4. Place the lamb kofta kebabs on the preheated grill and cook for about 6-8 minutes, turning occasionally, until they are cooked through and nicely browned on all sides.
5. Remove the kebabs from the grill and let them rest for a few minutes before serving.
6. Serve the Lamb Kofta Kebabs hot with your choice of dipping sauce or as a part of a larger meal with pita bread.

Lamb Tagine

Prep Time: 20 minutes / Cook time: 2 hours
Serves: 4 servings

Ingredients:

- 800g lamb shoulder, cut into chunks
- 2 tablespoons olive oil
- 1 onion, finely chopped
- 3 cloves garlic, minced
- 2 carrots, peeled and sliced
- 2 tomatoes, diced
- 1 tablespoon tomato paste
- 1 teaspoon ground cumin
- 1 teaspoon ground coriander
- 1 teaspoon ground cinnamon
- 1/2 teaspoon ground turmeric
- 1/2 teaspoon paprika

- Salt and pepper to taste
- 500ml lamb or vegetable broth
- 1 preserved lemon, sliced (optional)
- Fresh cilantro, chopped (for garnish)

Instructions:

1. Heat the olive oil in a large pot or tagine over medium heat. Add the chopped onion and minced garlic, and sauté until they become soft and translucent.
2. Add the lamb shoulder chunks to the pot and brown them on all sides.
3. Stir in the sliced carrots, diced tomatoes, tomato paste, ground cumin, ground coriander, ground cinnamon, ground turmeric, paprika, salt, and pepper. Mix well to coat the lamb and vegetables with the spices.
4. Pour in the lamb or vegetable broth to the pot. If using the preserved lemon, add the slices to the pot as well.
5. Cover the pot or tagine and let it simmer on low heat for about 1.5 to 2 hours, or until the lamb is tender and the flavours have melded together.
6. Taste and adjust the seasoning if needed.
7. Garnish with freshly chopped cilantro before serving.
8. Serve the Lamb Tagine hot with couscous or bread.

Turkey Meatballs in Tomato Sauce

Prep Time: 30 minutes / Cook time: 30 minutes
Serves: 4 servings

Ingredients:

- 500g ground turkey
- 60g breadcrumbs
- 30g grated Parmesan cheese
- 15g chopped fresh parsley
- 1 egg, lightly beaten
- 2 cloves garlic, minced
- 1 teaspoon dried oregano
- 1/2 teaspoon dried basil
- Salt and pepper to taste
- 30ml olive oil
- 1 onion, finely chopped
- 2 cloves garlic, minced
- 400g can diced tomatoes
- 15g tomato paste
- 1 teaspoon sugar
- Fresh basil leaves, chopped (for garnish)

Instructions:

1. In a large mixing bowl, combine the ground turkey, breadcrumbs, grated Parmesan cheese, chopped fresh parsley, lightly beaten egg, minced garlic, dried oregano, dried basil, salt, and pepper. Mix well until all the ingredients are evenly incorporated.
2. Shape the turkey mixture into meatballs of desired size.
3. Heat the olive oil in a large skillet over medium heat. Add the chopped onion and minced garlic, and sauté

until they become soft and translucent.
4. Add the meatballs to the skillet and cook until browned on all sides.
5. In a separate saucepan, combine the diced tomatoes, tomato paste, and sugar. Cook over medium heat until the sauce thickens slightly, about 10 minutes.
6. Pour the tomato sauce over the meatballs in the skillet. Reduce the heat to low, cover, and simmer for 15-20 minutes, or until the meatballs are cooked through.
7. Garnish with freshly chopped basil before serving.
8. Serve the Turkey Meatballs in Tomato Sauce hot with pasta, rice, or crusty bread.

Grilled Turkey Breast with Herb Butter

Prep Time: 15 minutes / Cook time: 25 minutes
Serves: 4 servings

Ingredients:

- 600g turkey breast, boneless and skinless
- 4 tablespoons unsalted butter, softened
- 2 cloves garlic, minced
- 1 tablespoon chopped fresh herbs (such as rosemary, thyme, or parsley)
- Salt and pepper to taste

Instructions:

1. Preheat the grill to medium-high heat.
2. In a small bowl, mix together the softened butter, minced garlic, chopped fresh herbs, salt, and pepper.
3. Season the turkey breast with salt and pepper on both sides.
4. Place the turkey breast on the preheated grill and cook for about 10-12 minutes per side, or until the internal temperature reaches 165°C (75°C) using a meat thermometer.
5. During the last few minutes of grilling, spread the herb butter mixture over the turkey breast, allowing it to melt and create a flavourful crust.
6. Remove the turkey breast from the grill and let it rest for a few minutes before slicing.
7. Slice the grilled turkey breast and serve it warm with your favourite side dishes.

Roast Venison with Red Wine Jus

Prep Time: 20 minutes / Cook time: 45 minutes
Serves: 4 servings

Ingredients:

- 800g venison roast
- 2 tablespoons olive oil
- Salt and pepper to taste
- 1 onion, chopped
- 2 cloves garlic, minced
- 250ml red wine
- 250ml beef or vegetable broth
- 2 tablespoons butter

- 2 tablespoons all-purpose flour
- Fresh herbs (such as rosemary or thyme) for garnish (optional)

Instructions:

1. Preheat the oven to 180°C.
2. Season the venison roast with salt and pepper on all sides.
3. Heat the olive oil in an oven-safe skillet or roasting pan over medium-high heat. Add the venison roast and sear it on all sides until browned.
4. Remove the seared venison roast from the skillet and set it aside.
5. In the same skillet, add the chopped onion and minced garlic. Sauté until the onion becomes translucent.
6. Deglaze the skillet by adding the red wine, scraping the bottom to release any browned bits. Let the wine simmer for a few minutes to reduce slightly.
7. Add the beef or vegetable broth to the skillet and bring it to a simmer.
8. Return the venison roast to the skillet and place it in the preheated oven.
9. Roast the venison for about 45 minutes to 1 hour, or until it reaches your desired level of doneness. The internal temperature should be around 55-60°C for medium-rare.
10. Remove the venison roast from the oven and transfer it to a cutting board. Cover it loosely with foil and let it rest for about 10 minutes before slicing.
11. Meanwhile, prepare the red wine jus. In a small saucepan, melt the butter over medium heat. Whisk in the flour to create a roux, and cook for a minute until it turns golden brown.
12. Slowly whisk in the juices from the roasting pan, straining out any solids, and bring the mixture to a simmer. Cook for a few minutes until the jus thickens slightly.
13. Slice the venison roast and serve it with the red wine jus. Garnish with fresh herbs, if desired.

Gammon Steak with Pineapple Salsa

Prep Time: 15 minutes / Cook time: 15 minutes
Serves: 2 servings

Ingredients:

- 2 gammon steaks
- Salt and pepper to taste
- 1 tablespoon olive oil

For the pineapple salsa:
- 50g diced fresh pineapple
- 1/2 red bell pepper, diced
- 1/2 red onion, finely chopped
- 1 jalapeño pepper, seeded and finely chopped
- Juice of 1 lime
- 1 tablespoon chopped fresh cilantro
- Salt to taste

Instructions:

1. Season the gammon steaks with salt and pepper on both sides.
2. Heat the olive oil in a skillet or grill pan over medium-high heat.
3. Cook the gammon steaks for about 4-5 minutes on each side, or until cooked through and nicely browned. The internal temperature should reach 70°C (160°F).
4. While the gammon steaks are cooking, prepare the pineapple salsa. In a bowl, combine the diced fresh pineapple, red bell pepper, red onion, jalapeño pepper, lime juice, chopped fresh cilantro, and salt. Mix well to combine.
5. Remove the gammon steaks from the skillet and let them rest for a few minutes.
6. Serve the gammon steaks hot, topped with the pineapple salsa.

Chicken and Wild Mushroom Pie

Prep Time: 20 minutes / Cook time: 50 minutes
Serves: 4-6 servings

Ingredients:

- 500 g boneless, skinless chicken breasts, cut into bite-sized pieces
- 200 g wild mushrooms (such as porcini, chanterelle, or shiitake), sliced
- 1 onion, diced
- 2 cloves garlic, minced
- 2 tablespoons butter
- 2 tablespoons all-purpose flour
- 250 ml chicken broth
- 120 ml heavy cream
- 1 teaspoon dried thyme
- Salt and pepper to taste
- 1 sheet puff pastry, thawed if frozen
- 1 egg, beaten (for egg wash)

Instructions:

1. Preheat the oven to 200°C.
2. In a large skillet, melt the butter over medium heat. Add the diced onion and minced garlic, and sauté until the onion is translucent and fragrant.
3. Add the chicken pieces to the skillet and cook until they are browned on all sides.
4. Add the sliced wild mushrooms to the skillet and cook for another 5 minutes, until the mushrooms are softened.
5. Sprinkle the flour over the chicken and mushrooms, stirring well to coat everything evenly.
6. Slowly pour in the chicken broth and heavy cream, stirring constantly to prevent lumps from forming. Bring the mixture to a simmer and cook for a few minutes until the sauce thickens.

7. Stir in the dried thyme, and season with salt and pepper to taste. Remove the skillet from the heat.
8. Transfer the chicken and mushroom mixture to a deep pie dish or individual ramekins.
9. Roll out the puff pastry sheet on a lightly floured surface to fit the top of the pie dish or ramekins. Place the pastry over the filling, pressing the edges to seal.
10. Brush the pastry with beaten egg to create a golden and glossy finish.
11. Cut a few small slits on the top of the pastry to allow steam to escape.
12. Place the pie dish or ramekins on a baking sheet and bake in the preheated oven for about 30 minutes, or until the pastry is puffed up and golden brown.
13. Remove from the oven and let the pie cool for a few minutes before serving.
14. Serve the chicken and wild mushroom pie hot, and enjoy the delicious combination of flavours and textures.

Chicken Cordon Bleu

Prep Time: 20 minutes / Cook time: 25 minutes
Serves: 4 servings

Ingredients:

- 4 boneless, skinless chicken breasts
- Salt and pepper to taste
- 4 slices Swiss cheese
- 4 slices ham
- 60g all-purpose flour
- 2 eggs, beaten
- 120g breadcrumbs
- 30ml olive oil

Instructions:

1. Preheat the oven to 200°C.
2. Place each chicken breast between two sheets of plastic wrap and pound them with a meat mallet until they are about 1/4-inch thick. Season the chicken breasts with salt and pepper.
3. Lay a slice of Swiss cheese and a slice of ham on top of each chicken breast.
4. Place the flour, beaten eggs, and breadcrumbs in separate shallow dishes.
5. Dredge each chicken breast in flour, dip it in beaten eggs, and coat it with breadcrumbs, pressing gently to adhere.
6. Heat olive oil in a large skillet over medium heat. Add the breaded chicken breasts and cook for about 3-4 minutes on each side, until golden brown.
7. Transfer the browned chicken breasts to a baking sheet and bake in the preheated oven for 15-20 minutes, or until the chicken is cooked through and the cheese is melted.
8. Remove from the oven and let the chicken rest for a

few minutes before serving.
9. Serve the chicken cordon bleu hot, accompanied by your favourite side dishes such as mashed potatoes and steamed vegetables.

Chicken Schnitzel with Lemon and Parsley

Prep Time: 15 minutes / Cook time: 15 minutes
Serves: 4 servings

Ingredients:

- 4 boneless, skinless chicken breasts
- Salt and pepper to taste
- 120 g all-purpose flour
- 2 eggs, beaten
- 200 g breadcrumbs
- 60g grated Parmesan cheese
- Zest of 1 lemon
- 30g fresh parsley, chopped
- 60ml vegetable oil
- Lemon wedges, for serving

Instructions:

1. Place each chicken breast between two sheets of plastic wrap and pound them with a meat mallet until they are about 1/4-inch thick. Season the chicken breasts with salt and pepper.
2. In separate shallow dishes, place the flour, beaten eggs, and a mixture of breadcrumbs, grated Parmesan cheese, lemon zest, and chopped parsley.
3. Dredge each chicken breast in flour, dip it in beaten eggs, and coat it with the breadcrumb mixture, pressing gently to adhere.
4. Heat vegetable oil in a large skillet over medium-high heat. Add the breaded chicken breasts and cook for about 3-4 minutes on each side, until golden brown and cooked through.
5. Remove the cooked chicken schnitzels from the skillet and place them on a paper towel-lined plate to drain excess oil.
6. Serve the chicken schnitzels hot, garnished with lemon wedges. They pair well with a side salad or your choice of vegetables.

Chicken Noodle Soup

Prep Time: 10 minutes / Cook time: 30 minutes
Serves: 4 servings

Ingredients:

- 2 chicken breasts, boneless and skinless
- Salt and pepper to taste
- 1 tablespoon olive oil
- 1 onion, diced
- 2 carrots, sliced
- 2 celery stalks, sliced
- 2 cloves garlic, minced
- 1 litre chicken broth

- 200g egg noodles
- 1 teaspoon dried thyme
- 1 bay leaf
- Fresh parsley, chopped (for garnish)

Instructions:

1. Season the chicken breasts with salt and pepper. In a large pot, heat olive oil over medium heat. Add the chicken breasts and cook until browned on both sides. Remove the chicken from the pot and set aside.
2. In the same pot, add the diced onion, sliced carrots, sliced celery, and minced garlic. Sauté for a few minutes until the vegetables start to soften.
3. Pour in the chicken broth and bring it to a boil. Reduce the heat to low and add the cooked chicken breasts back to the pot.
4. Simmer for about 20 minutes until the chicken is cooked through and tender. Remove the chicken from the pot and shred it into bite-sized pieces using two forks. Set aside.
5. Meanwhile, cook the egg noodles according to the package instructions in a separate pot. Drain and set aside.
6. Remove the bay leaf from the soup. Return the shredded chicken and cooked noodles to the pot.
7. Season the soup with dried thyme, salt, and pepper to taste. Stir well to combine and let the soup simmer for another 5 minutes to allow the flavours to meld together.
8. Serve the chicken noodle soup hot, garnished with fresh chopped parsley. It's a comforting and satisfying meal on its own or paired with crusty bread.

Chicken and Broccoli Alfredo Pasta

Prep Time: 10 minutes / Cook time: 20 minutes
Serves: 4 servings

Ingredients:

- 300g chicken breast, cut into bite-sized pieces
- Salt and pepper to taste
- 250g broccoli florets
- 250 g fettuccine pasta
- 30ml olive oil
- 2 cloves garlic, minced
- 200ml heavy cream
- 60g grated Parmesan cheese
- Fresh parsley, chopped (for garnish)

Instructions:

1. Season the chicken breast with salt and pepper. In a large skillet, heat olive oil over medium-high heat. Add the chicken and cook until browned and cooked through. Remove the chicken from the skillet and set aside.
2. In the same skillet, add the minced garlic and cook for about 1 minute until fragrant. Add the broccoli florets and sauté for a few minutes until slightly tender.

3. Cook the fettuccine pasta according to the package instructions until al dente. Drain and set aside.
4. Pour the heavy cream into the skillet with the garlic and broccoli. Bring it to a simmer and let it cook for a couple of minutes to thicken slightly.
5. Stir in the grated Parmesan cheese and cooked chicken. Cook for an additional 2-3 minutes until the sauce is creamy and well combined.
6. Add the cooked fettuccine pasta to the skillet and toss everything together until the pasta is well coated with the sauce.
7. Season with additional salt and pepper if needed. Garnish with fresh chopped parsley.
8. Serve the chicken and broccoli Alfredo pasta hot, and enjoy the delicious combination of flavours.

Chicken and Bacon Carbonara

Prep Time: 10 minutes / Cook time: 20 minutes
Serves: 4 servings

Ingredients:

- 250g spaghetti pasta
- -200g chicken breast, cut into bite-sized pieces
- 150g bacon, chopped
- 2 cloves garlic, minced
- 3 egg yolks
- 60g grated Parmesan cheese
- Salt and pepper to taste
- Fresh parsley, chopped (for garnish)

Instructions:

1. Cook the spaghetti pasta according to the package instructions until al dente. Drain and set aside.
2. In a large skillet, cook the chopped bacon until crispy. Remove the bacon from the skillet and set aside on a paper towel-lined plate.
3. In the same skillet, add the minced garlic and cook for about 1 minute until fragrant. Add the chicken breast pieces and cook until browned and cooked through.
4. In a small bowl, whisk together the egg yolks and grated Parmesan cheese. Season with salt and pepper.
5. Add the cooked spaghetti pasta to the skillet with the chicken and garlic. Pour the egg and Parmesan mixture over the pasta, quickly tossing everything together to coat the pasta evenly.
6. Cook for an additional 2-3 minutes until the sauce thickens slightly and coats the pasta.
7. Remove from heat and sprinkle the crispy bacon over the top. Garnish with fresh chopped parsley.
8. Serve the chicken and bacon carbonara hot, and enjoy the creamy and flavourful dish.

Chicken and Bacon Ranch Pasta Salad

Prep Time: 15 minutes / Cook time: 15 minutes
Serves: 6 servings

Ingredients:

- 250g rotini pasta
- 200g chicken breast, cooked and diced
- 150g bacon, cooked and crumbled
- 100g cherry tomatoes, halved
- 1/2 red onion, finely chopped
- 1/2 cucumber, diced
- 60g shredded cheddar cheese
- 60g ranch dressing
- 30 g fresh parsley, chopped
- Salt and pepper to taste

Instructions:

1. Cook the rotini pasta according to the package instructions until al dente. Drain and rinse with cold water to cool.
2. In a large mixing bowl, combine the cooked and diced chicken breast, crumbled bacon, halved cherry tomatoes, finely chopped red onion, diced cucumber, and shredded cheddar cheese.
3. Add the cooled rotini pasta to the bowl and mix everything together.
4. Pour the ranch dressing over the pasta salad and toss well to coat all the ingredients evenly. Adjust the amount of dressing to your liking.
5. Season with salt and pepper to taste. Sprinkle fresh chopped parsley over the top for added freshness and flavour.
6. Cover the bowl and refrigerate for at least 1 hour to allow the flavours to meld together.
7. Serve the chicken and bacon ranch pasta salad chilled as a delicious and satisfying meal on its own or as a side dish at gatherings and picnics.

Grilled Turkey Burgers with Cranberry Relish

Prep Time: 15 minutes / Cook time: 12 minutes
Serves: 4 servings

Ingredients:

- For the turkey burgers:
- 500g ground turkey
- 30g breadcrumbs
- 40g finely chopped onion
- 2 cloves garlic, minced
- 1 teaspoon dried thyme
- 1 teaspoon dried sage
- 1/2 teaspoon salt
- 1/4 teaspoon black pepper
- 4 burger buns
- Lettuce leaves and sliced tomatoes for garnish

For the cranberry relish:
- 200g cranberries, fresh or frozen
- 10ml orange juice
- 2 tablespoons honey
- 1/4 teaspoon ground cinnamon
- Pinch of salt

Instructions:

1. Preheat the grill to medium-high heat.
2. In a mixing bowl, combine the ground turkey, breadcrumbs, chopped onion, minced garlic, dried thyme, dried sage, salt, and black pepper. Mix well until all the ingredients are evenly incorporated.
3. Divide the turkey mixture into 4 equal portions and shape them into patties.
4. Place the turkey patties on the preheated grill and cook for about 6 minutes per side, or until the internal temperature reaches 165°C. Make sure to flip the patties gently to prevent them from breaking.
5. While the turkey burgers are cooking, prepare the cranberry relish. In a saucepan, combine the cranberries, orange juice, honey, ground cinnamon, and salt. Cook over medium heat for about 10 minutes, or until the cranberries burst and the mixture thickens slightly. Stir occasionally.
6. Remove the turkey burgers from the grill and let them rest for a few minutes.
7. Toast the burger buns on the grill for a minute or until lightly toasted.
8. Assemble the turkey burgers by placing each patty on a toasted bun. Top with a spoonful of cranberry relish, lettuce leaves, and sliced tomatoes.
9. Serve the grilled turkey burgers with cranberry relish immediately and enjoy the juicy and flavourful combination.

Beef and Broccoli Teriyaki

Prep Time: 15 minutes / Cook time: 20 minutes
Serves: 4 servings

Ingredients:

- 400g beef sirloin or flank steak, thinly sliced
- 2 tablespoons soy sauce
- 2 tablespoons teriyaki sauce
- 1 tablespoon honey
- 2 cloves garlic, minced
- 1 teaspoon grated ginger
- 2 tablespoons vegetable oil
- 1 head broccoli, cut into florets
- 120ml beef broth or water
- 1 tablespoon cornstarch mixed with 2 tablespoons water
- Sesame seeds and sliced green onions for garnish
- Cooked rice for serving

Instructions:

1. In a bowl, combine the soy sauce, teriyaki sauce, honey, minced garlic, and grated ginger. Mix well to make the teriyaki sauce.
2. Place the thinly sliced beef in a separate bowl and pour half of the teriyaki sauce over it. Toss to coat the beef evenly and let it marinate for about 10 minutes.
3. Heat the vegetable oil in a large skillet or wok over

medium-high heat. Add the marinated beef slices and stir-fry for 2-3 minutes until browned and cooked through. Remove the beef from the skillet and set it aside.

4. In the same skillet, add the broccoli florets and stir-fry for 2 minutes. Pour in the beef broth or water, cover the skillet, and cook for an additional 2-3 minutes until the broccoli is tender-crisp.

5. Return the cooked beef to the skillet with the broccoli. Pour in the remaining teriyaki sauce and stir to combine.

6. In a small bowl, mix the cornstarch with water to make a slurry. Pour the slurry into the skillet and stir well to thicken the sauce. Cook for another minute until the sauce is glossy and thickened.

7. Remove the beef and broccoli teriyaki from the heat. Garnish with sesame seeds and sliced green onions.

8. Serve the beef and broccoli teriyaki over cooked rice and enjoy this flavourful and satisfying dish.

Pork Tenderloin Medallions with Creamy Mustard Sauce

Prep Time: 10 minutes / Cook time: 20 minutes
Serves: 4 servings

Ingredients:

- 500g pork tenderloin, cut into medallions
- Salt and pepper to taste
- 2 tablespoons olive oil
- 2 cloves garlic, minced
- 120g chicken broth
- 100g heavy cream
- 2 tablespoons Dijon mustard
- 1 tablespoon whole grain mustard
- 1 tablespoon chopped fresh parsley (for garnish)

Instructions:

1. Season the pork tenderloin medallions with salt and pepper on both sides.

2. Heat the olive oil in a large skillet over medium-high heat. Add the pork medallions to the skillet and cook for about 4-5 minutes per side, or until they are browned and cooked through. Remove the pork medallions from the skillet and set them aside.

3. In the same skillet, add the minced garlic and sauté for about 1 minute until fragrant.

4. Pour in the chicken broth and deglaze the skillet, scraping up any browned bits from the bottom.

5. Reduce the heat to medium and add the heavy cream, Dijon mustard, and whole grain mustard to the skillet. Stir well to combine and let the sauce simmer for a few minutes until it thickens slightly.

6. Return the pork medallions to the skillet and coat them with the creamy mustard sauce. Cook for an additional minute to heat the medallions through and allow the flavours to meld.

7. Remove the pork medallions from the skillet and transfer them to a serving plate. Spoon the creamy mustard sauce over the medallions.

8. Garnish with chopped fresh parsley.

9. Serve the pork tenderloin medallions with creamy mustard sauce alongside your choice of sides, such as roasted vegetables or mashed potatoes, for a delicious and satisfying meal.

Pork Chops with Cider Glaze

Prep Time: 10 minutes / Cook time: 20 minutes
Serves: 4 servings

Ingredients:

- 4 bone-in pork chops
- Salt and pepper to taste
- 2 tablespoons vegetable oil
- 120ml apple cider or apple juice
- 2 tablespoons Dijon mustard
- 2 tablespoons maple syrup
- 1 tablespoon apple cider vinegar
- Chopped fresh parsley for garnish

Instructions:

1. Season the pork chops with salt and pepper on both sides.

2. Heat the vegetable oil in a large skillet over medium-high heat. Add the pork chops to the skillet and cook for about 4-5 minutes per side, or until they are browned and cooked through. Remove the pork chops from the skillet and set them aside.

3. In the same skillet, pour in the apple cider or apple juice. Bring it to a simmer and let it cook for a few minutes to reduce slightly.

4. Stir in the Dijon mustard, maple syrup, and apple cider vinegar. Continue to simmer the sauce for another couple of minutes until it thickens slightly.

5. Return the pork chops to the skillet and coat them with the cider glaze. Cook for an additional minute to heat the chops through and allow the flavours to meld.

6. Remove the pork chops from the skillet and transfer them to a serving plate. Drizzle any remaining glaze over the chops.

7. Garnish with chopped fresh parsley.

Beef and Black Bean Stir-Fry

Prep Time: 15 minutes / Cook time: 15 minutes
Serves: 4 servings

Ingredients:

- 500g beef steak, thinly sliced
- 2 tablespoons vegetable oil
- 2 cloves garlic, minced
- 1 tablespoon grated ginger
- 1 red bell pepper, thinly sliced
- 1 green bell pepper, thinly sliced

- 1 small onion, thinly sliced
- 1 can black beans, drained and rinsed
- 3 tablespoons soy sauce
- 2 tablespoons oyster sauce
- 1 tablespoon hoisin sauce
- 1 teaspoon sesame oil
- Salt and pepper to taste
- Spring onions, sliced (for garnish)
- Cooked rice or noodles (for serving)

Instructions:

1. In a large wok or skillet, heat the vegetable oil over high heat. Add the minced garlic and grated ginger, and stir-fry for about 1 minute until fragrant.
2. Add the sliced beef to the wok and stir-fry for 2-3 minutes until it is browned and cooked to your desired doneness. Remove the beef from the wok and set it aside.
3. In the same wok, add the sliced bell peppers and onion. Stir-fry for about 3-4 minutes until the vegetables are slightly tender.
4. Add the black beans to the wok and stir-fry for another minute to heat them through.
5. In a small bowl, whisk together the soy sauce, oyster sauce, hoisin sauce, and sesame oil. Pour the sauce mixture into the wok and stir to coat the vegetables and beans.
6. Return the cooked beef to the wok and toss everything together. Cook for another minute to allow the flavours to meld and the beef to reheat.
7. Season with salt and pepper to taste. Garnish with sliced spring onions.
8. Serve the beef and black bean stir-fry over cooked rice or noodles for a delicious and satisfying meal.

Lamb Souvlaki with Tzatziki Sauce

Prep Time: 15 minutes / Cook time: 10 minutes
Serves: 4 servings

Ingredients:

- 500g lamb shoulder or leg, cut into cubes
- 2 tablespoons olive oil
- 2 cloves garlic, minced
- 1 tablespoon dried oregano
- 1 teaspoon ground cumin
- Juice of 1 lemon
- Salt and pepper to taste
- 4 pita breads
- Tzatziki sauce (store-bought or homemade)
- Sliced tomatoes, cucumbers, and red onions

Instructions:

1. In a bowl, combine the olive oil, minced garlic, dried oregano, ground cumin, lemon juice, salt, and pepper. Stir well to create a marinade.
2. Add the lamb cubes to the marinade and toss to coat them evenly. Cover the bowl and let the lamb

marinate in the refrigerator for at least 1 hour or overnight for maximum flavour.
3. Preheat a grill or grill pan over medium-high heat.
4. Thread the marinated lamb cubes onto skewers. If using wooden skewers, soak them in water for 15 minutes beforehand to prevent them from burning.
5. Grill the lamb skewers for about 4-5 minutes per side, or until they are cooked to your desired doneness.
6. While the lamb is grilling, warm the pita breads on the grill for about 1 minute on each side.
7. Once the lamb is cooked, remove it from the skewers and transfer it to a serving platter.

Air Fryer Orange Chicken with Rice

Prep Time: 15 minutes / Cook time: 15minutes
Serves: 4 servings

Ingredients:

- 4 boneless, skinless chicken breasts, cut into 1 inch pieces
- 200 g flour
- 2 tsp paprika
- 2 tsp garlic powder
- Salt and pepper, to taste
- 2 eggs, beaten
- 200 g Panko breadcrumbs
- 2 tbsp olive oil
- 1 orange, zested and juiced
- 2 garlic cloves, minced
- 2 tbsp ginger, grated
- 2 tbsp honey
- 2 tbsp soy sauce
- 1 tsp sesame oil
- 1 tbsp cornstarch
- 60 ml water
- 200 g long-grain rice, cooked

Ingredients:

1. In a shallow dish, mix together flour, paprika, garlic powder, salt, and pepper.
2. In another shallow dish, beat the eggs.
3. In a third shallow dish, mix together Panko breadcrumbs.
4. Dip chicken pieces into the flour mixture, then the eggs, and finally the Panko mixture to coat well.
5. Place chicken pieces in a single layer in the basket of an air fryer and drizzle with 2 tablespoons of olive oil.
6. Air fry at 180°C for 10-12 minutes or until crispy and fully cooked.
7. In a saucepan, heat the orange juice, orange zest, garlic, ginger, honey, soy sauce, and sesame oil over medium heat.
8. In a small bowl, mix the cornstarch and water together. Add the mixture to the saucepan and stir to combine.
9. Cook the sauce for 2-3 minutes or until thickened.
10. Serve the air fryer chicken pieces over a bed of cooked rice and top with the orange sauce. Enjoy!

Chapter 5 Beans and Legumes Recipes

Classic Baked Beans on Toast

Prep Time: 5 minutes / Cook time: 15 minutes
Serves: 2 servings

Ingredients:

- 400g can of baked beans
- 2 slices of bread
- Butter or margarine (for spreading)
- Optional toppings: grated cheese, chopped parsley, hot sauce

Instructions:

1. Heat the baked beans in a saucepan over medium heat. Stir occasionally and cook for about 10 minutes, or until heated through.
2. While the baked beans are cooking, toast the bread slices until golden brown.
3. Spread butter or margarine on the toasted bread slices.
4. Once the baked beans are heated, spoon them over the buttered toast.
5. Optional: Sprinkle grated cheese on top of the baked beans and melt it under the grill or in the microwave for a minute.
6. Garnish with chopped parsley and drizzle with hot sauce, if desired.
7. Serve the classic baked beans on toast as a delicious and quick meal for breakfast, lunch, or dinner.

Spicy Chickpea Curry

Prep Time: 10 minutes / Cook time: 25 minutes
Serves: 4 servings

Ingredients:

- 2 tablespoons vegetable oil
- 1 onion, finely chopped
- 2 cloves garlic, minced
- 1 tablespoon grated ginger
- 1 teaspoon ground cumin
- 1 teaspoon ground coriander
- 1/2 teaspoon turmeric powder
- 1/2 teaspoon chilli powder (adjust to taste)
- 400g can of chickpeas, drained and rinsed
- 400g can of diced tomatoes
- 200ml coconut milk
- Salt and pepper to taste
- Fresh cilantro leaves (for garnish)
- Cooked rice or naan bread (for serving)

Instructions:

1. Heat the vegetable oil in a large skillet or pan over medium heat. Add the chopped onion and sauté for about 5 minutes until softened and translucent.
2. Add the minced garlic and grated ginger to the skillet and sauté for an additional 1-2 minutes until fragrant.
3. Stir in the ground cumin, ground coriander, turmeric powder, and chilli powder. Cook for about 1 minute to toast the spices and release their flavours.
4. Add the drained and rinsed chickpeas, diced tomatoes (with their juices), and coconut milk to the skillet. Stir well to combine.
5. Bring the mixture to a simmer and let it cook for about 15 minutes, stirring occasionally, to allow the flavours to meld and the sauce to thicken slightly. If needed, add a splash of water to adjust the consistency.
6. Season the spicy chickpea curry with salt and pepper to taste.
7. Garnish with fresh cilantro leaves.
8. Serve the spicy chickpea curry over cooked rice or with naan bread for a satisfying and flavourful vegetarian meal.

Curried Lentil and Cauliflower Soup

Prep Time: 10 minutes / Cook time: 30 minutes
Serves: 4 servings

Ingredients:

- 200g red lentils
- 1 medium cauliflower, cut into florets
- 1 medium onion, chopped
- 2 cloves garlic, minced
- 1 tablespoon curry powder
- 1 teaspoon ground cumin
- 1 teaspoon ground turmeric
- 1/2 teaspoon ground coriander
- 960ml vegetable broth
- 240ml coconut milk
- 15ml olive oil

Instructions:

1. Rinse the red lentils under cold water and set aside.
2. In a large pot, heat the olive oil over medium heat. Add the chopped onion and minced garlic. Sauté for about 5 minutes until the onion is softened and translucent.
3. Add the curry powder, ground cumin, ground turmeric, and ground coriander to the pot. Stir well to coat the onions and garlic with the spices. Cook for 1-2 minutes to toast the spices and enhance their flavours.
4. Add the red lentils, cauliflower florets, vegetable broth, and coconut milk to the pot. Stir to combine all the ingredients.
5. Bring the soup to a boil, then reduce the heat to low.

Cover the pot and let the soup simmer for about 20-25 minutes, or until the lentils and cauliflower are tender.
6. Season the soup with salt and pepper to taste. Adjust the seasoning according to your preference.
7. Use an immersion blender or transfer the soup to a blender, and blend until smooth and creamy.
8. Serve the curried lentil and cauliflower soup hot, garnished with fresh chopped cilantro.

Red Lentil Dahl

Prep Time: 10 minutes / Cook time: 30 minutes
Serves: 4 servings

Ingredients:

- 200g red lentils, rinsed
- 1 onion, finely chopped
- 2 cloves garlic, minced
- 1 tablespoon grated ginger
- 1 teaspoon ground cumin
- 1 teaspoon ground coriander
- 1/2 teaspoon turmeric powder
- 1/2 teaspoon chilli powder (adjust to taste)
- 400g can of diced tomatoes
- 400ml vegetable broth or water
- 200ml coconut milk
- Juice of 1/2 lemon
- Salt to taste
- Fresh cilantro leaves (for garnish)
- Cooked rice or naan bread (for serving)

Instructions:

1. In a large saucepan, heat a little oil over medium heat. Add the chopped onion and sauté for about 5 minutes until softened and translucent.
2. Add the minced garlic and grated ginger to the saucepan and sauté for an additional 1-2 minutes until fragrant.
3. Stir in the ground cumin, ground coriander, turmeric powder, and chilli powder. Cook for about 1 minute to toast the spices and release their flavours.
4. Add the rinsed red lentils, diced tomatoes (with their juices), and vegetable broth or water to the saucepan. Stir well to combine.
5. Bring the mixture to a boil, then reduce the heat to low. Cover the saucepan and let the lentils simmer for about 20-25 minutes, or until they are tender and cooked through.
6. Stir in the coconut milk and lemon juice. Simmer for an additional 5 minutes to allow the flavours to meld together.
7. Season the red lentil dahl with salt to taste.
8. Garnish with fresh cilantro leaves.
9. Serve the red lentil dahl over cooked rice or with naan bread for a comforting and satisfying vegetarian meal.

Butterbean and Vegetable Casserole

Prep Time: 15 minutes / Cook time: 45 minutes
Serves: 4 servings

Ingredients:

- 400g can butter beans, drained and rinsed
- 1 onion, chopped
- 2 cloves garlic, minced
- 2 carrots, diced
- 2 celery stalks, diced
- 1 red bell pepper, diced
- 200g mushrooms, sliced
- 400g can diced tomatoes
- 250ml vegetable broth
- 2 tablespoons tomato paste
- 1 teaspoon dried thyme
- 1 teaspoon dried oregano
- 1/2 teaspoon paprika
- Salt and pepper to taste
- Fresh parsley, chopped (for garnish)

Instructions:

1. Preheat the oven to 180°C (350°F).
2. In a large oven-safe pot or casserole dish, heat some oil over medium heat. Add the chopped onion and minced garlic and cook until fragrant and translucent.
3. Add the diced carrots, celery, red bell pepper, and mushrooms to the pot. Cook for a few minutes until the vegetables start to soften.
4. Stir in the butterbeans, diced tomatoes, vegetable broth, tomato paste, dried thyme, dried oregano, and paprika. Season with salt and pepper to taste. Mix well to combine all the ingredients.
5. Cover the pot or casserole dish and transfer it to the preheated oven. Bake for about 40-45 minutes, or until the vegetables are tender and the flavours have melded together.
6. Remove from the oven and garnish with freshly chopped parsley.
7. Serve the butterbean and vegetable casserole as a comforting and nutritious main dish. It pairs well with crusty bread or rice.

Mexican Black Bean Soup

Prep Time: 15 minutes / Cook time: 30 minutes
Serves: 4 servings

Ingredients:

- 2 cans (400g each) black beans, drained and rinsed
- 1 onion, chopped
- 2 cloves garlic, minced
- 1 red bell pepper, diced
- 1 jalapeño pepper, seeded and minced (optional for spice)
- 1 can (400g) diced tomatoes

- 500ml vegetable broth
- 2 teaspoons chilli powder
- 1 teaspoon ground cumin
- 1/2 teaspoon smoked paprika
- 1/2 teaspoon dried oregano
- Juice of 1 lime
- Salt and pepper to taste
- Fresh cilantro, chopped (for garnish)
- Sour cream or Greek yoghourt (for serving, optional)

Instructions:

1. In a large pot, heat some oil over medium heat. Add the chopped onion and minced garlic. Sauté until the onion is translucent and fragrant.
2. Add the diced red bell pepper and jalapeño pepper (if using) to the pot. Cook for a few minutes until the peppers are slightly softened.
3. Stir in the black beans, diced tomatoes, vegetable broth, chilli powder, ground cumin, smoked paprika, and dried oregano. Season with salt and pepper to taste. Mix well to combine all the ingredients.
4. Bring the soup to a boil, then reduce the heat to low. Cover the pot and let it simmer for about 20-25 minutes to allow the flavours to develop.
5. Using an immersion blender or a countertop blender, blend the soup until smooth and creamy. If using a countertop blender, work in batches and be careful when blending hot liquids.
6. Stir in the lime juice and adjust the seasoning if needed.
7. Serve the Mexican black bean soup hot, garnished with fresh cilantro. You can also add a dollop of sour cream or Greek yoghourt on top if desired.

Smoky Three Bean chilli

Prep Time: 15 minutes / Cook time: 40 minutes
Serves: 4 servings

Ingredients:

- 200g kidney beans, soaked overnight and cooked until tender
- 200g black beans, soaked overnight and cooked until tender
- 200g pinto beans, soaked overnight and cooked until tender
- 1 onion, chopped
- 2 cloves garlic, minced
- 1 red bell pepper, diced
- 1 jalapeño pepper, seeded and minced (optional for spice)
- 400g can diced tomatoes
- 250ml vegetable broth
- 2 tablespoons tomato paste
- 2 teaspoons smoked paprika
- 1 teaspoon ground cumin

- 1 teaspoon chilli powder
- 1/2 teaspoon dried oregano
- Salt and pepper to taste
- Fresh cilantro, chopped (for garnish)
- Lime wedges (for serving)

Instructions:

1. In a large pot, heat some oil over medium heat. Add the chopped onion and minced garlic. Sauté until the onion is translucent and fragrant.
2. Add the diced red bell pepper and jalapeño pepper (if using) to the pot. Cook for a few minutes until the peppers are slightly softened.
3. Stir in the cooked kidney beans, black beans, and pinto beans. Add the diced tomatoes, vegetable broth, tomato paste, smoked paprika, ground cumin, chilli powder, dried oregano, salt, and pepper. Mix well to combine all the ingredients.
4. Bring the chilli to a boil, then reduce the heat to low. Cover the pot and let it simmer for about 30-40 minutes to allow the flavours to meld together.
5. Adjust the seasoning if needed and add more liquid if desired.
6. Serve the smoky three bean chilli hot, garnished with fresh cilantro. Squeeze a lime wedge over each serving for an extra burst of freshness.

Tuscan White Bean Soup

Prep Time: 15 minutes / Cook time: 40 minutes
Serves: 4 servings

Ingredients:

- 200g dried cannellini beans, soaked overnight and cooked until tender
- 1 onion, chopped
- 2 cloves garlic, minced
- 2 carrots, diced
- 2 celery stalks, diced
- 1 medium potato, peeled and diced
- 400g can diced tomatoes
- 1 litre vegetable broth
- 2 teaspoons dried rosemary
- 1 teaspoon dried thyme
- 1 bay leaf
- Salt and pepper to taste
- Fresh parsley, chopped (for garnish)
- Extra virgin olive oil (for drizzling)

Instructions:

1. In a large pot, heat some oil over medium heat. Add the chopped onion and minced garlic. Sauté until the onion is translucent and fragrant.
2. Add the diced carrots, celery, and potato to the pot. Cook for a few minutes until the vegetables start to soften.
3. Stir in the cooked cannellini beans, diced tomatoes,

vegetable broth, dried rosemary, dried thyme, bay leaf, salt, and pepper. Mix well to combine all the ingredients.

4. Bring the soup to a boil, then reduce the heat to low. Cover the pot and let it simmer for about 30-40 minutes, or until the vegetables are tender and the flavours have melded together.

5. Remove the bay leaf and adjust the seasoning if needed.

6. Serve the Tuscan white bean soup hot, garnished with fresh parsley and a drizzle of extra virgin olive oil.

Lentil and Vegetable Curry

Prep Time: 15 minutes / Cook time: 30 minutes
Serves: 4 servings

Ingredients:

- 200g red lentils, rinsed
- 1 onion, chopped
- 2 cloves garlic, minced
- 1 carrot, diced
- 1 red bell pepper, diced
- 1 zucchini, diced
- 400g can diced tomatoes
- 400ml coconut milk
- 2 tablespoons curry powder
- 1 teaspoon ground cumin
- 1 teaspoon ground coriander
- 1/2 teaspoon turmeric
- 1/2 teaspoon paprika
- Salt and pepper to taste
- Fresh cilantro, chopped (for garnish)
- Cooked rice or naan bread (for serving)

Instructions:

1. In a large pot, heat some oil over medium heat. Add the chopped onion and minced garlic. Sauté until the onion is translucent and fragrant.

2. Add the diced carrot, red bell pepper, and zucchini to the pot. Cook for a few minutes until the vegetables start to soften.

3. Stir in the rinsed red lentils, diced tomatoes, coconut milk, curry powder, ground cumin, ground coriander, turmeric, paprika, salt, and pepper. Mix well to combine all the ingredients.

4. Bring the curry to a boil, then reduce the heat to low. Cover the pot and let it simmer for about 20-30 minutes, or until the lentils are cooked and the vegetables are tender.

5. Adjust the seasoning if needed and add more liquid if desired.

6. Serve the lentil and vegetable curry hot, garnished with fresh cilantro. Serve with cooked rice or naan bread for a complete meal.

Spicy Black Bean Burgers

Prep Time: 15 minutes / Cook time: 10 minutes
Serves: 4 servings

Ingredients:

- 400g can black beans, drained and rinsed
- 1/2 onion, chopped
- 2 cloves garlic, minced
- 1/2 red bell pepper, diced
- 1/2 jalapeño pepper, seeded and minced (optional for spice)
- 30g breadcrumbs
- 35g cornmeal
- 1 teaspoon ground cumin
- 1 teaspoon chilli powder
- 1/2 teaspoon paprika
- Salt and pepper to taste
- 2 tablespoons vegetable oil
- Burger buns
- Toppings of choice (lettuce, tomato, onion, etc.)

Instructions:

1. In a large mixing bowl, mash the black beans with a fork or potato masher until they are mostly mashed but still have some texture.

2. Add the chopped onion, minced garlic, diced red bell pepper, minced jalapeño pepper (if using), breadcrumbs, cornmeal, ground cumin, chilli powder, paprika, salt, and pepper to the bowl. Mix well to combine all the ingredients.

3. Shape the mixture into patties of your desired size.

4. Heat vegetable oil in a skillet over medium heat. Cook the black bean patties for about 4-5 minutes per side, or until they are golden brown and heated through.

5. Toast the burger buns if desired. Place a black bean patty on each bun and top with your favourite toppings.

6. Serve the spicy black bean burgers hot as a delicious vegetarian option for your next burger night.

Chickpea and Spinach Stew

Prep Time: 10 minutes / Cook time: 25 minutes
Serves: 4 servings

Ingredients:

- 1 tablespoon olive oil
- 1 onion, chopped
- 3 cloves garlic, minced
- 1 red bell pepper, diced
- 1 carrot, diced
- 1 teaspoon ground cumin
- 1 teaspoon ground coriander
- 1/2 teaspoon turmeric
- 1/2 teaspoon paprika
- 1/4 teaspoon cayenne pepper (optional for heat)

- 240g canned chickpeas, drained and rinsed
- 400g canned diced tomatoes
- 200ml vegetable broth
- 200g fresh spinach
- Salt and pepper to taste
- Fresh cilantro, chopped (for garnish)
- Cooked rice or crusty bread (for serving)

Instructions:

1. Heat olive oil in a large pot over medium heat. Add the chopped onion and minced garlic. Sauté until the onion is translucent and fragrant.
2. Add the diced red bell pepper and carrot to the pot. Cook for a few minutes until the vegetables start to soften.
3. Stir in the ground cumin, ground coriander, turmeric, paprika, and cayenne pepper (if using). Mix well to coat the vegetables with the spices.
4. Add the drained and rinsed chickpeas, diced tomatoes, and vegetable broth to the pot. Bring the mixture to a simmer and let it cook for about 15 minutes, allowing the flavours to blend together.
5. Stir in the fresh spinach and cook for another 5 minutes, or until the spinach wilts.
6. Season the stew with salt and pepper to taste.
7. Serve the chickpea and spinach stew hot, garnished with fresh cilantro. Serve with cooked rice or crusty bread for a hearty and nutritious meal.

Smoky Chipotle Black Bean Soup

Prep Time: 10 minutes / Cook time: 30 minutes
Serves: 4 servings

Ingredients:

- 15g olive oil
- 1 onion, chopped
- 2 cloves garlic, minced
- 2 teaspoons ground cumin
- 1 teaspoon smoked paprika
- 1 teaspoon chipotle powder
- 400g canned black beans, drained and rinsed
- 400g canned diced tomatoes
- 500ml vegetable broth
- 1 tablespoon lime juice
- Salt and pepper to taste
- Fresh cilantro, chopped (for garnish)
- Sour cream or vegan yoghourt (optional, for serving)

Instructions:

1. Heat olive oil in a large pot over medium heat. Add the chopped onion and minced garlic. Sauté until the onion is translucent and fragrant.
2. Stir in the ground cumin, smoked paprika, and chipotle powder. Cook for a minute to toast the spices.
3. Add the drained and rinsed black beans, diced tomatoes, and vegetable broth to the pot. Bring the

mixture to a boil, then reduce the heat and let it simmer for about 20 minutes to allow the flavours to meld together.
4. Using an immersion blender or regular blender, blend about half of the soup until smooth. This step is optional but helps to create a thicker consistency.
5. Stir in the lime juice and season the soup with salt and pepper to taste.
6. Serve the smoky chipotle black bean soup hot, garnished with fresh cilantro. You can also add a dollop of sour cream or vegan yoghourt if desired.

Vegan Lentil Sloppy Joes

Prep Time: 10 minutes / Cook time: 25 minutes
Serves: 4 servings

Ingredients:

- 15g olive oil
- 1 onion, finely chopped
- 2 cloves garlic, minced
- 1 red bell pepper, finely chopped
- 200g brown lentils, cooked and drained
- 240ml tomato sauce
- 2 tablespoons tomato paste
- 1 tablespoon maple syrup or agave nectar
- 2 tablespoons soy sauce or tamari
- 1 teaspoon smoked paprika
- 1/2 teaspoon chilli powder
- Salt and pepper to taste
- Hamburger buns or bread rolls
- Optional toppings: sliced pickles, sliced onions, lettuce, vegan cheese

Instructions:

1. Heat olive oil in a large skillet or pan over medium heat. Add the chopped onion, minced garlic, and diced red bell pepper. Sauté until the vegetables are softened and lightly browned.
2. Stir in the cooked and drained lentils, tomato sauce, tomato paste, maple syrup or agave nectar, soy sauce or tamari, smoked paprika, and chilli powder. Mix well to combine all the ingredients.
3. Reduce the heat to low and let the mixture simmer for about 15 minutes, allowing the flavours to meld together. Stir occasionally to prevent sticking.
4. Season the lentil mixture with salt and pepper to taste.
5. Serve the vegan lentil sloppy joes on hamburger buns or bread rolls. Add your desired toppings such as sliced pickles, sliced onions, lettuce, or vegan cheese.

Moroccan Chickpea Stew

Prep Time: 15 minutes / Cook time: 30 minutes
Serves: 4 servings

Ingredients:

- 15ml olive oil
- 1 onion, diced
- 3 cloves garlic, minced
- 5ml ground cumin
- 5ml ground coriander
- 2.5ml ground turmeric
- 2.5ml ground cinnamon
- 1ml cayenne pepper (optional, for heat)
- 2 carrots, peeled and diced
- 1 red bell pepper, diced
- 1 can (400 g) diced tomatoes
- 480ml vegetable broth
- 2 cans (400 g each) chickpeas, drained and rinsed
- 60g dried apricots, chopped
- 30g raisins
- Salt and pepper to taste
- Fresh cilantro or parsley, chopped (for garnish)

Instructions:

1. Heat olive oil in a large pot over medium heat. Add the diced onion and minced garlic to the pot. Sauté for 3-4 minutes until the onion is translucent and fragrant.
2. Add the ground cumin, ground coriander, ground turmeric, ground cinnamon, and cayenne pepper (if using) to the pot. Stir well to coat the onions and garlic with the spices. Cook for an additional 1-2 minutes to toast the spices.
3. Add the diced carrots and diced red bell pepper to the pot. Stir and cook for 5 minutes until the vegetables begin to soften.
4. Pour in the diced tomatoes (including the liquid) and vegetable broth. Stir to combine.
5. Add the drained and rinsed chickpeas, chopped dried apricots, and raisins to the pot. Stir to incorporate all the ingredients.
6. Bring the stew to a boil, then reduce the heat to low. Cover the pot and simmer for 20-25 minutes, until the flavours meld together and the stew thickens slightly.
7. Season with salt and pepper to taste.
8. Serve the Moroccan Chickpea Stew hot, garnished with fresh cilantro or parsley.

Chickpea and Vegetable Stir-Fry

Prep Time: 15 minutes / Cook time: 15 minutes
Serves: 4 servings

Ingredients:

- 200g canned chickpeas, drained and rinsed
- 1 red bell pepper, sliced
- 1 yellow bell pepper, sliced
- 1 zucchini, sliced
- 1 carrot, julienned
- 50g broccoli florets
- 3 cloves garlic, minced
- 2 tablespoons soy sauce or tamari
- 1 tablespoon sesame oil
- 1 tablespoon rice vinegar
- 1 tablespoon maple syrup or agave nectar
- 1/2 teaspoon ground ginger
- 2 tablespoons chopped fresh cilantro (optional, for garnish)
- Sesame seeds (optional, for garnish)

Instructions:

1. Heat sesame oil in a large skillet or wok over medium-high heat. Add the minced garlic and cook for about 1 minute until fragrant.
2. Add the sliced red bell pepper, sliced yellow bell pepper, sliced zucchini, julienned carrot, and broccoli florets to the skillet. Stir-fry the vegetables for about 5-7 minutes until they are tender-crisp.
3. In a small bowl, whisk together the soy sauce or tamari, rice vinegar, maple syrup or agave nectar, and ground ginger to make the sauce.
4. Pour the sauce over the stir-fried vegetables in the skillet. Add the drained and rinsed chickpeas to the skillet as well. Stir everything together to coat the vegetables and chickpeas with the sauce.
5. Continue to cook for another 2-3 minutes, allowing the flavours to blend together.
6. Remove the skillet from heat and garnish with chopped fresh cilantro and sesame seeds if desired.
7. Serve the chickpea and vegetable stir-fry as a main dish with rice or noodles, or as a side dish with your favourite protein.

Lentil and Sweet Potato Curry

Prep Time: 15 minutes / Cook time: 30 minutes
Serves: 4 servings

Ingredients:

- 15ml vegetable oil
- 1 onion, diced
- 3 cloves garlic, minced
- 2.5ml fresh ginger, grated
- 5ml ground cumin
- 5ml ground coriander
- 2.5ml ground turmeric
- 2.5ml ground cinnamon
- 2.5ml red pepper flakes (adjust to taste)
- 2 medium sweet potatoes, peeled and diced
- 240g dried red lentils, rinsed
- 480ml vegetable broth
- 1 can (400 g) diced tomatoes
- 240ml coconut milk
- Salt and pepper to taste

- Fresh cilantro, chopped (for garnish)

Instructions:

1. Heat vegetable oil in a large pot over medium heat. Add the diced onion, minced garlic, and grated ginger. Sauté for 3-4 minutes until the onion is soft and fragrant.
2. Add the ground cumin, ground coriander, ground turmeric, ground cinnamon, and red pepper flakes to the pot. Stir well to coat the onions and spices. Cook for an additional 1-2 minutes to toast the spices.
3. Add the diced sweet potatoes, red lentils, vegetable broth, and diced tomatoes (including the liquid) to the pot. Stir to combine all the ingredients.
4. Bring the mixture to a boil, then reduce the heat to low. Cover the pot and simmer for 20-25 minutes, or until the lentils and sweet potatoes are tender.
5. Stir in the coconut milk and season with salt and pepper to taste. Simmer for an additional 5 minutes to heat through.
6. Serve the Lentil and Sweet Potato Curry hot, garnished with fresh cilantro. Enjoy with rice or naan bread.

Spicy Mexican Pinto Beans

Prep Time: 10 minutes / Cook time: 25 minutes
Serves: 4 servings

Ingredients:

- 15ml vegetable oil
- 1 onion, diced
- 2 cloves garlic, minced
- 1 jalapeño pepper, seeded and finely chopped
- 5ml ground cumin
- 5ml chilli powder
- 2.5ml paprika
- 1 can (400 g) pinto beans, drained and rinsed
- 240ml vegetable broth
- 1 can (400 g) diced tomatoes
- Salt and pepper to taste
- Fresh cilantro, chopped (for garnish)
- Lime wedges (for serving)

Instructions:

1. Heat vegetable oil in a large skillet over medium heat. Add the diced onion, minced garlic, and chopped jalapeño pepper. Sauté for 3-4 minutes until the onion is soft and the jalapeño is fragrant.
2. Add the ground cumin, chilli powder, and paprika to the skillet. Stir well to coat the onions and spices. Cook for an additional 1-2 minutes to toast the spices.
3. Add the pinto beans, vegetable broth, and diced tomatoes (including the liquid) to the skillet. Stir to combine all the ingredients.
4. Bring the mixture to a boil, then reduce the heat to low. Cover the skillet and simmer for 20 minutes, stirring occasionally, until the flavours meld together.

5. Season with salt and pepper to taste.
6. Serve the Spicy Mexican Pinto Beans hot, garnished with fresh cilantro.

Harissa Roasted Chickpeas

Prep Time: 5 minutes / Cook time: 25 minutes
Serves: 4 servings

Ingredients:

- 400g canned chickpeas, drained and rinsed
- 15ml olive oil
- 5g harissa paste
- 2.5g ground cumin
- 2.5g paprika
- 2.5g salt
- Fresh cilantro, chopped (for garnish)

Instructions:

1. Preheat the oven to 200°C.
2. In a bowl, combine the chickpeas, olive oil, harissa paste, ground cumin, paprika, and salt. Toss well to coat the chickpeas evenly.
3. Spread the chickpeas in a single layer on a baking sheet.
4. Roast in the preheated oven for 20-25 minutes, or until the chickpeas are crispy and golden brown, shaking the baking sheet halfway through to ensure even cooking.
5. Remove from the oven and let the chickpeas cool slightly.
6. Serve the Harissa Roasted Chickpeas warm, garnished with fresh cilantro. Enjoy as a snack or as a topping for salads and bowls.

Spicy Mexican Refried Beans

Prep Time: 10 minutes / Cook time: 20 minutes
Serves: 4-6

Ingredients:

- 400g cooked pinto beans
- 1 tablespoon vegetable oil
- 1 small onion, finely chopped
- 2 cloves garlic, minced
- 1 teaspoon cumin powder
- 1/2 teaspoon chilli powder (adjust to taste)
- 1/2 teaspoon paprika
- 1/4 teaspoon cayenne pepper (optional for extra heat)
- Salt to taste
- 60g water (or more as needed)
- Fresh cilantro leaves, chopped (for garnish)

Instructions:

1. Heat vegetable oil in a pan over medium heat. Add the chopped onion and minced garlic. Sauté until the onion becomes soft and translucent, about 3-4 minutes.

2. Add the cumin powder, chilli powder, paprika, cayenne pepper (if using), and salt to the pan. Stir well to combine the spices with the onion and garlic mixture.
3. Add the cooked pinto beans to the pan and mash them using a potato masher or fork until they are mostly mashed but still have some texture.
4. Pour water into the pan and stir to combine. Cook the mixture for about 10 minutes, stirring occasionally, until the beans are heated through and the flavours have melded together. Add more water if needed to achieve your desired consistency.
5. Adjust the seasoning if necessary and remove from heat.
6. Serve the Spicy Mexican Refried Beans hot, garnished with fresh cilantro leaves. They are delicious as a side dish or as a filling for burritos, tacos, or quesadillas.

Smoky Bean and Vegetable Casserole

Prep Time: 15 minutes / Cook time: 45 minutes
Serves: 4-6

Ingredients:

- 400g mixed beans (such as kidney beans, black beans, and cannellini beans), cooked and drained
- 1 tablespoon vegetable oil
- 1 onion, chopped
- 2 cloves garlic, minced
- 1 red bell pepper, diced
- 1 zucchini, diced
- 1 carrot, diced
- 1 can diced tomatoes (400 g)
- 1 tablespoon tomato paste
- 1 teaspoon smoked paprika
- 1 teaspoon ground cumin
- 1/2 teaspoon chilli powder (adjust to taste)
- Salt and pepper to taste
- 240ml vegetable broth or water
- Fresh parsley or cilantro, chopped (for garnish)

Instructions:

1. Preheat the oven to 180°C.
2. Heat vegetable oil in a large oven-safe pan or casserole dish over medium heat.
3. Add the chopped onion and minced garlic to the pan. Sauté until the onion becomes soft and translucent, about 3-4 minutes.
4. Add the diced red bell pepper, zucchini, and carrot to the pan. Cook for another 5 minutes until the vegetables start to soften.
5. Stir in the diced tomatoes, tomato paste, smoked paprika, ground cumin, chilli powder, salt, and pepper. Mix well to combine the spices with the vegetables.
6. Add the cooked mixed beans and vegetable broth (or

water) to the pan. Stir to combine all the ingredients.
7. Cover the pan with a lid or foil and transfer it to the preheated oven. Bake for 30-35 minutes, or until the vegetables are tender and the flavours have melded together
8. Remove from the oven and let it cool slightly before serving.
9. Garnish with fresh parsley or cilantro.
10. Serve the Smoky Bean and Vegetable Casserole hot as a main dish or as a side with crusty bread or rice.

Lentil and Mushroom Burgers

Prep Time: 20 minutes / Cook time: 15 minutes
Serves: 4 burgers

Ingredients:

- 200g cooked lentils
- 200g mushrooms, finely chopped
- 1 small onion, finely chopped
- 2 cloves garlic, minced
- 1 teaspoon cumin powder
- 1 teaspoon smoked paprika
- 1/2 teaspoon dried thyme
- 1/2 teaspoon salt
- 1/4 teaspoon black pepper
- 2 tablespoons soy sauce
- 2 tablespoons tomato paste
- 2 tablespoons breadcrumbs
- 2 tablespoons olive oil
- Burger buns and desired toppings for serving

Instructions:

1. In a large mixing bowl, mash the cooked lentils using a fork or potato masher until they are partially mashed but still have some texture.
2. Heat 1 tablespoon of olive oil in a pan over medium heat. Add the chopped mushrooms and cook for about 5 minutes until they release their moisture and start to brown. Remove the mushrooms from the pan and set aside.
3. In the same pan, add another tablespoon of olive oil and sauté the chopped onion and minced garlic until they become soft and translucent, about 3-4 minutes.
4. Add the cooked mushrooms to the pan with the onions and garlic. Stir in the cumin powder, smoked paprika, dried thyme, salt, and black pepper. Cook for an additional 2 minutes to allow the flavours to meld together.
5. Transfer the mushroom and onion mixture to the bowl with the mashed lentils. Add the soy sauce, tomato paste, and breadcrumbs. Mix well until all the ingredients are combined.
6. Divide the mixture into 4 portions and shape each portion into a patty using your hands. Press the patties firmly to hold their shape.

7. Heat a non-stick pan or grill pan over medium heat. Brush the pan with a little olive oil. Place the lentil and mushroom patties in the pan and cook for about 5-6 minutes on each side, or until they are browned and heated through.
8. Once the lentil and mushroom burgers are cooked, remove them from the pan and let them rest for a few minutes.
9. Serve the Lentil and Mushroom Burgers on burger buns with your favorite toppings, such as lettuce, tomato slices, onion, and condiments of your choice.

Chickpea and Tomato Curry

Prep Time: 10 minutes / Cook time: 25 minutes
Serves: 4 servings

Ingredients:

- 400g canned chickpeas, drained and rinsed
- 1 tablespoon vegetable oil
- 1 medium onion, diced
- 3 cloves garlic, minced
- 1 tablespoon ginger, grated
- 1 teaspoon ground cumin
- 1 teaspoon ground coriander
- 1 teaspoon turmeric
- 1/2 teaspoon paprika
- 1/4 teaspoon cayenne pepper (optional for added heat)
- 400g canned diced tomatoes
- 200ml coconut milk
- Salt and pepper to taste
- Fresh cilantro, chopped (for garnish)
- Cooked rice or naan bread (for serving)

Instructions:

1. Heat the vegetable oil in a large pan over medium heat. Add the diced onion and cook until softened and translucent, about 5 minutes.
2. Add the minced garlic and grated ginger to the pan and cook for an additional 1-2 minutes, until fragrant.
3. Stir in the ground cumin, ground coriander, turmeric, paprika, and cayenne pepper (if using). Cook for about 1 minute to toast the spices and release their flavours.
4. Add the canned diced tomatoes and their juices to the pan. Stir well to combine with the spices and bring the mixture to a simmer.
5. Add the drained and rinsed chickpeas to the pan, stirring them into the tomato mixture. Allow the curry to simmer for 10-15 minutes, allowing the flavours to meld together and the sauce to thicken slightly.
6. Pour in the coconut milk and stir well. Continue to simmer for another 5 minutes, until the curry is heated through.
7. Season with salt and pepper to taste. Adjust the spice level by adding more cayenne pepper if desired.

8. Remove the pan from the heat and garnish the Chickpea and Tomato Curry with freshly chopped cilantro.
9. Serve the curry over cooked rice or with warm naan bread for a complete and satisfying meal.

Black Eyed Pea Salad with Avocado and Lime Dressing

Prep Time: 15 minutes / Cook time: 10 minutes
Serves: 4 servings

Ingredients:

- 250g dried black-eyed peas
- 1 large avocado, diced
- 1 medium red bell pepper, diced
- 1 small red onion, finely chopped
- 1 jalapeno pepper, seeds removed and finely chopped
- 1 small bunch fresh cilantro, chopped
- Juice of 2 limes
- 30ml olive oil
- Salt and pepper to taste

Instructions:

1. Rinse the dried black-eyed peas under cold water and drain. Place them in a pot and cover with water. Bring to a boil, then reduce the heat to a simmer and cook for about 10 minutes, or until the peas are tender but still hold their shape. Drain and set aside to cool.
2. In a large bowl, combine the diced avocado, red bell pepper, red onion, jalapeno pepper, and chopped cilantro.
3. In a separate small bowl, whisk together the lime juice, olive oil, salt, and pepper to make the dressing.
4. Add the cooked black-eyed peas to the bowl with the avocado and vegetables. Pour the lime dressing over the mixture and gently toss to combine, ensuring all ingredients are evenly coated.
5. Taste and adjust the seasoning if needed.
6. Cover the bowl and refrigerate for at least 30 minutes to allow the flavours to meld together.
7. Serve the Black Eyed Pea Salad chilled as a side dish or light lunch. It can be enjoyed on its own or paired with grilled meats, fish, or as a topping for salads.

Lentil and Spinach Curry

Prep Time: 10 minutes / Cook time: 30 minutes
Serves: 4 servings

Ingredients:

- 200g dried lentils
- 200g fresh spinach leaves
- 1 medium onion, chopped
- 2 cloves garlic, minced
- 1 medium tomato, chopped
- 400ml coconut milk
- 15ml vegetable oil

- 5g curry powder
- 5g ground cumin
- 5g ground coriander
- 2g turmeric
- Salt to taste
- Fresh cilantro, chopped (for garnish)

Instructions:

1. Rinse the lentils under cold water and drain well. Set aside.
2. Heat the vegetable oil in a large pot or deep skillet over medium heat. Add the chopped onion and minced garlic, and sauté until the onion becomes soft and translucent.
3. Add the curry powder, ground cumin, ground coriander, and turmeric to the pot. Stir well to coat the onions and garlic with the spices, and let them cook for about a minute to release their flavours.
4. Add the chopped tomato to the pot and cook for a few minutes until it starts to break down.
5. Add the rinsed lentils to the pot, along with enough water to cover them. Bring to a boil, then reduce the heat to low and let it simmer for about 20-25 minutes, or until the lentils are tender.
6. Stir in the coconut milk and fresh spinach leaves. Cook for an additional 5 minutes, or until the spinach wilts down and the flavours meld together.
7. Season with salt to taste. Adjust the seasoning and thickness of the curry according to your preference by adding more water or coconut milk if needed.
8. Remove from heat and let the Lentil and Spinach Curry sit for a few minutes to allow the flavours to meld together.
9. Serve the curry warm, garnished with fresh cilantro. It pairs well with rice, naan bread, or any other preferred accompaniments.

Butterbean and Tomato Stew

Prep Time: 10 minutes / Cook time: 30 minutes
Serves: 4 servings

Ingredients:

- 400g canned butterbeans, drained and rinsed
- 400g canned diced tomatoes
- 1 medium onion, chopped
- 2 cloves garlic, minced
- 1 medium carrot, diced
- 1 medium red bell pepper, diced
- 250ml vegetable broth
- 15ml olive oil
- 5g dried oregano
- 5g paprika
- Salt and pepper to taste
- Fresh parsley, chopped (for garnish)

Instructions:

1. Heat the olive oil in a large pot over medium heat. Add the chopped onion and minced garlic and sauté until the onion is translucent and fragrant.
2. Add the diced carrot and red bell pepper to the pot and continue to cook for a few minutes until the vegetables start to soften.
3. Add the canned diced tomatoes (with their juices) to the pot, along with the vegetable broth, dried oregano, and paprika. Stir well to combine.
4. Season with salt and pepper to taste. Bring the stew to a boil, then reduce the heat to low and let it simmer for about 20 minutes, allowing the flavours to meld together.
5. Add the drained and rinsed butterbeans to the pot and stir gently to incorporate them into the stew. Cook for an additional 5-10 minutes to heat the beans through.
6. Remove the stew from the heat and let it cool slightly. Serve the Butterbean and Tomato Stew warm, garnished with fresh parsley.

Chapter 6 Healthy Vegetables and Sides

Air-Fried Parmesan Courgette Fries

Prep Time: 15 minutes / Cook time: 15 minutes
Serves: 4

Ingredients:

- 4 medium courgettes (approximately 500g)
- 50g panko breadcrumbs
- 25g grated Parmesan cheese
- 1 tsp garlic powder
- 1/2 tsp dried oregano
- 1/2 tsp paprika
- 1/4 tsp salt
- Freshly ground black pepper, to taste
- Cooking spray

Instructions:

1. Preheat the air fryer to 200°C for 5 minutes.
2. Cut the courgettes into long, thin fries, approximately 1.5cm wide and 8-10cm long.
3. In a shallow bowl, combine the panko breadcrumbs, grated Parmesan cheese, garlic powder, dried oregano, paprika, salt, and black pepper.
4. Working in batches, dip the courgette fries into the breadcrumb mixture, pressing gently to adhere the coating.
5. Place the coated courgette fries in a single layer in the air fryer basket. Lightly spray them with cooking spray.
6. Air fry the courgette fries at 200°C for 12-15 minutes, or until golden and crispy, flipping them halfway through the cooking time for even browning.
7. Once cooked, remove the courgette fries from the air fryer and serve immediately as a healthy and delicious snack or side dish.

Air-Fried Mediterranean Vegetables

Prep Time: 15 minutes / Cook time: 10 minutes
Serves: 4

Ingredients:

- 1 red pepper, sliced
- 1 yellow pepper, sliced
- 1 small aubergine, diced
- 1 courgette, sliced
- 1 red onion, sliced
- 2 cloves of garlic, minced
- 2 tbsp olive oil
- 1 tsp dried oregano
- 1 tsp dried basil
- 1/2 tsp dried thyme
- Salt and black pepper, to taste
- Fresh parsley, chopped (for garnish)

Instructions:

1. Preheat the air fryer to 200°C for 5 minutes.
2. In a large mixing bowl, combine the sliced red and yellow peppers, diced aubergine, sliced courgette, red onion, and minced garlic.
3. Drizzle the vegetables with olive oil and sprinkle with dried oregano, dried basil, dried thyme, salt, and black pepper. Toss until well-coated.
4. Place the seasoned vegetables in the air fryer basket in a single layer. If necessary, cook them in batches to avoid overcrowding.
5. Air fry the vegetables at 200°C for 12-15 minutes, shaking the basket halfway through the cooking time to ensure even cooking.
6. Once the vegetables are tender and slightly caramelised, remove them from the air fryer and transfer them to a serving dish.
7. Garnish with fresh parsley and serve hot as a delicious and healthy side dish.

Garlic Parmesan Broccoli

Prep Time: 10 minutes / Cook time: 12 minutes
Serves: 4

Ingredients:

- 500g broccoli florets
- 2 tbsp olive oil
- 2 cloves of garlic, minced
- 1/4 cup grated Parmesan cheese
- 1/2 tsp dried oregano
- 1/2 tsp dried basil
- Salt and black pepper, to taste
- Lemon wedges, for serving (optional)

Instructions:

1. Preheat the air fryer to 200°C for 5 minutes.
2. In a large mixing bowl, combine the broccoli florets, olive oil, minced garlic, grated Parmesan cheese, dried oregano, dried basil, salt, and black pepper. Toss until the broccoli is evenly coated.
3. Place the seasoned broccoli florets in the air fryer basket in a single layer. If necessary, cook them in batches to avoid overcrowding.
4. Air fry the broccoli at 200°C for 10-12 minutes, shaking the basket or tossing the broccoli halfway through the cooking time to ensure even cooking and

browning.

5. Once the broccoli is tender and lightly browned, remove it from the air fryer and transfer it to a serving dish.

6. Serve the air-fried garlic Parmesan broccoli hot as a nutritious side dish. Squeeze fresh lemon juice over the broccoli, if desired, for a bright and tangy flavour.

Spicy Sweet Potato Wedges

Prep Time: 10 minutes / Cook time: 20 minutes
Serves: 4

Ingredients:

- 4 medium sweet potatoes
- 2 tbsp olive oil
- 1 tsp smoked paprika
- 1/2 tsp ground cumin
- 1/2 tsp garlic powder
- 1/4 tsp cayenne pepper (adjust to taste)
- Salt and black pepper, to taste
- Fresh parsley or coriander, chopped (for garnish)

Instructions:

1. Preheat the air fryer to 200°C for 5 minutes.
2. Wash and scrub the sweet potatoes. Cut them into wedges of approximately equal thickness.
3. In a large mixing bowl, combine the olive oil, smoked paprika, ground cumin, garlic powder, cayenne pepper, salt, and black pepper. Stir until well-mixed.
4. Add the sweet potato wedges to the bowl and toss until evenly coated with the spice mixture.
5. Place the seasoned sweet potato wedges in the air fryer basket in a single layer. If necessary, cook them in batches to avoid overcrowding.
6. Air fry the sweet potato wedges at 200°C for 15-20 minutes, flipping them halfway through the cooking time to ensure even browning.
7. Once the sweet potato wedges are crispy and golden brown, remove them from the air fryer and transfer them to a serving dish.
8. Garnish with fresh parsley or coriander and serve the spicy sweet potato wedges hot as a delightful and healthy snack or side dish.

Brussels Sprouts with Balsamic Glaze

Prep Time: 10 minutes / Cook time: 15 minutes
Serves: 4

Ingredients:

- 500g Brussels sprouts, trimmed and halved
- 2 tbsp olive oil
- 2 tbsp balsamic vinegar
- 1 tbsp honey
- Salt and black pepper, to taste
- Grated Parmesan cheese, for garnish (optional)

Instructions:

1. Preheat the air fryer to 200°C for 5 minutes.
2. In a large mixing bowl, combine the Brussels sprouts, olive oil, balsamic vinegar, honey, salt, and black pepper. Toss until the Brussels sprouts are evenly coated.
3. Place the seasoned Brussels sprouts in the air fryer basket in a single layer. If necessary, cook them in batches to avoid overcrowding.
4. Air fry the Brussels sprouts at 200°C for 12-15 minutes, shaking the basket or tossing the sprouts halfway through the cooking time for even browning.
5. Once the Brussels sprouts are tender and caramelised, remove them from the air fryer and transfer them to a serving dish.
6. Optional: Sprinkle the air-fried Brussels sprouts with grated Parmesan cheese for added flavour and richness.
7. Serve the air-fried Brussels sprouts with balsamic glaze hot as a delectable and healthy side dish.

Air-Fried Cauliflower Buffalo Bites

Prep Time: 15 minutes / Cook time: 15 minutes
Serves: 4

Ingredients:

- 1 medium cauliflower head, cut into florets
- 65 g plain flour
- 120 mlmilk (or plant-based milk)
- 1 tsp garlic powder
- 1 tsp paprika
- 1/2 tsp salt
- 1/4 tsp black pepper
- 60 g hot sauce (such as Frank's RedHot Sauce)
- 2 tbsp melted butter (or plant-based butter)
- Ranch or blue cheese dressing, for dipping

Instructions:

1. Preheat the air fryer to 200°C for 5 minutes.
2. In a mixing bowl, combine the flour, milk, garlic powder, paprika, salt, and black pepper to make a batter.
3. Dip the cauliflower florets into the batter, coating them evenly, and allowing any excess batter to drip off.
4. Place the battered cauliflower florets in the air fryer basket in a single layer. If necessary, cook them in batches to avoid overcrowding.
5. Air fry the cauliflower at 200°C for 12-15 minutes, or until golden and crispy, flipping them halfway through the cooking time.
6. In a separate bowl, mix the hot sauce and melted butter to create the buffalo sauce.
7. Once the cauliflower bites are cooked, transfer them to a mixing bowl and toss them with the buffalo sauce until evenly coated.

8. Serve the air-fried cauliflower buffalo bites hot with ranch or blue cheese dressing on the side for dipping.

Carrot Fries

Prep Time: 10 minutes / Cook time: 15 minutes
Serves: 4

Ingredients:

- 500g carrots, cut into thin fries
- 2 tbsp olive oil
- 1 tsp paprika
- 1/2 tsp garlic powder
- 1/2 tsp onion powder
- 1/2 tsp dried thyme
- Salt and black pepper, to taste
- Fresh parsley, chopped (for garnish)

Instructions:

1. Preheat the air fryer to 200°C for 5 minutes.
2. In a large mixing bowl, combine the carrot fries, olive oil, paprika, garlic powder, onion powder, dried thyme, salt, and black pepper. Toss until the carrot fries are evenly coated.
3. Place the seasoned carrot fries in the air fryer basket in a single layer. If necessary, cook them in batches to avoid overcrowding.
4. Air fry the carrot fries at 200°C for 12-15 minutes, shaking the basket or tossing the fries halfway through the cooking time for even browning.
5. Once the carrot fries are crispy and golden brown, remove them from the air fryer and transfer them to a serving dish.
6. Garnish with fresh parsley and serve the air-fried carrot fries hot as a nutritious and tasty side dish.

Butternut Squash Chips

Prep Time: 15 minutes / Cook time: 20 minutes
Serves: 4

Ingredients:

- 1 medium butternut squash
- 2 tbsp olive oil
- 1 tsp smoked paprika
- 1/2 tsp garlic powder
- 1/2 tsp dried rosemary
- 1/4 tsp salt
- 1/4 tsp black pepper

Instructions:

1. Preheat the air fryer to 200°C for 5 minutes.
2. Peel the butternut squash, remove the seeds, and cut it into thin slices or chips.
3. In a large mixing bowl, combine the butternut squash slices, olive oil, smoked paprika, garlic powder, dried rosemary, salt, and black pepper. Toss until the butternut squash slices are well-coated.

4. Place the seasoned butternut squash slices in the air fryer basket in a single layer. If necessary, cook them in batches to avoid overcrowding.
5. Air fry the butternut squash chips at 200°C for 18-20 minutes, flipping them halfway through the cooking time for even browning.
6. Once the butternut squash chips are crispy and lightly browned, remove them from the air fryer and transfer them to a serving dish.

Aubergine Parmesan

Prep Time: 20 minutes / Cook time: 20 minutes
Serves: 4

Ingredients:

- 1 large aubergine, sliced into 1 cm rounds
- Salt
- 100g breadcrumbs
- 50g grated Parmesan cheese
- 1/2 tsp dried oregano
- 1/2 tsp dried basil
- 1/4 tsp garlic powder
- 2 eggs, beaten
- 200g marinara sauce
- 100g shredded mozzarella cheese
- Fresh basil leaves, for garnish

Instructions:

1. Preheat the air fryer to 200°C for 5 minutes.
2. Sprinkle salt on both sides of the aubergine slices and let them sit for 10 minutes to draw out excess moisture. Pat dry with a paper towel.
3. In a shallow bowl, combine the breadcrumbs, grated Parmesan cheese, dried oregano, dried basil, and garlic powder.
4. Dip each aubergine slice into the beaten eggs, allowing any excess to drip off, then coat them in the breadcrumb mixture.
5. Place the breaded aubergine slices in the air fryer basket in a single layer. If necessary, cook them in batches to avoid overcrowding.
6. Air fry the aubergine slices at 200°C for 10 minutes, flip them over, and continue air frying for an additional 10 minutes, or until golden and crisp.
7. Remove the air-fried aubergine slices from the air fryer and transfer them to a baking dish.
8. Spoon marinara sauce over each slice and top with shredded mozzarella cheese.
9. Place the baking dish with the topped aubergine slices under a grill or in the air fryer for 2-3 minutes, or until the cheese is melted and bubbly.

Air-Fried Green Bean Fries

Prep Time: 10 minutes / Cook time: 12 minutes
Serves: 4

Ingredients:

- 400g green beans, ends trimmed
- 2 eggs, beaten
- 100g breadcrumbs
- 50g grated Parmesan cheese
- 1/2 tsp garlic powder
- 1/2 tsp smoked paprika
- 1/4 tsp salt
- 1/4 tsp black pepper
- Cooking spray

Instructions:

1. Preheat the air fryer to 200°C for 5 minutes.
2. In a shallow bowl, combine the breadcrumbs, grated Parmesan cheese, garlic powder, smoked paprika, salt, and black pepper.
3. Dip each green bean into the beaten eggs, allowing any excess to drip off, then coat it in the breadcrumb mixture.
4. Place the breaded green beans in the air fryer basket in a single layer. If necessary, cook them in batches to avoid overcrowding.
5. Lightly coat the green beans with cooking spray to promote browning.
6. Air fry the green bean fries at 200°C for 10-12 minutes, shaking the basket or flipping the fries halfway through the cooking time for even browning.
7. Once the green bean fries are golden brown and crisp, remove them from the air fryer and transfer them to a serving dish.

Stuffed Peppers

Prep Time: 15 minutes / Cook time: 20 minutes
Serves: 4

Ingredients:

- 4 peppers (any colour)
- 200g cooked quinoa
- 200g cooked black beans
- 1 small onion, finely chopped
- 2 cloves garlic, minced
- 1 tsp ground cumin
- 1 tsp paprika
- 1/2 tsp dried oregano
- Salt and black pepper, to taste
- 100g grated cheddar cheese
- Fresh coriander, for garnish

Instructions:

1. Preheat the air fryer to 180°C for 5 minutes.
2. Cut the tops off the peppers and remove the seeds and membranes.
3. In a large mixing bowl, combine the cooked quinoa, black beans, chopped onion, minced garlic, ground cumin, paprika, dried oregano, salt, and black pepper. Mix well.
4. Stuff each bell pepper with the quinoa and black bean mixture, pressing it down gently.
5. Place the stuffed peppers in the air fryer basket.
6. Air fry the stuffed peppers at 180°C for 18-20 minutes, or until the peppers are tender and slightly charred.
7. Sprinkle the grated cheddar cheese on top of each stuffed pepper and air fry for an additional 2-3 minutes, until the cheese is melted and bubbly.
8. Remove the air-fried stuffed peppers from the air fryer and garnish with fresh coriander.

Stuffed Portobello Mushrooms

Prep Time: 15 minutes / Cook time: 15 minutes
Serves: 4

Ingredients:

- 4 large portobello mushrooms
- 200g spinach, chopped
- 1 small onion, finely chopped
- 2 cloves garlic, minced
- 100g feta cheese, crumbled
- 2 tbsp olive oil
- 1 tsp dried oregano
- Salt and black pepper, to taste
- Fresh parsley, for garnish

Instructions:

1. Preheat the air fryer to 180°C for 5 minutes.
2. Remove the stems from the portobello mushrooms and gently scrape out the gills with a spoon.
3. In a large skillet, heat 1 tablespoon of olive oil over medium heat. Add the chopped onion and minced garlic, and sauté until the onion becomes translucent.
4. Add the chopped spinach to the skillet and cook until wilted. Season with salt, black pepper, and dried oregano. Remove from heat.
5. In a bowl, combine the sautéed spinach mixture with the crumbled feta cheese. Mix well.
6. Brush the mushroom caps with the remaining olive oil, both on the inside and outside.
7. Fill each mushroom cap with the spinach and feta mixture, pressing it down gently.
8. Place the stuffed portobello mushrooms in the air fryer basket.
9. Air fry the stuffed mushrooms at 180°C for 12-15 minutes, or until the mushrooms are tender and the filling is heated through.
10. Remove the air-fried stuffed portobello mushrooms from the air fryer and garnish with fresh parsley.

Air-Fried Baked Potatoes

Prep Time: 5 minutes / Cook time: 40 minutes
Serves: 4

Ingredients:

• 4 medium-sized baking potatoes
• 1 tablespoon olive oil
• Salt, to taste
• Toppings of your choice (e.g., sour cream, chives, shredded cheese)

Instructions:

1. Preheat the air fryer to 200°C for 5 minutes.
2. Scrub the baking potatoes clean and pat them dry with a kitchen towel.
3. Pierce each potato several times with a fork to allow steam to escape during cooking.
4. Rub the potatoes with olive oil, ensuring they are evenly coated.
5. Sprinkle salt all over the potatoes, according to your taste preferences.
6. Place the potatoes in the air fryer basket in a single layer, ensuring they have enough space for air circulation.
7. Air fry the potatoes at 200°C for 35-40 minutes, or until they are tender and the skin is crispy.
8. Once the potatoes are cooked, carefully remove them from the air fryer.
9. Allow the potatoes to cool for a few minutes before handling.
10. Slice the potatoes open lengthwise, and fluff the insides with a fork.
11. Add your desired toppings, such as sour cream, chives, or shredded cheese.

Cauliflower "Steaks"

Prep Time: 10 minutes / Cook time: 15 minutes
Serves: 4

Ingredients:

• 1 large head of cauliflower
• 2 tablespoons olive oil
• 1 teaspoon garlic powder
• 1/2 teaspoon paprika
• 1/2 teaspoon dried thyme
• 1/2 teaspoon salt
• 1/4 teaspoon black pepper
• Optional toppings: fresh herbs (parsley or coriander), lemon wedges

Instructions:

1. Preheat the air fryer to 200°C for 5 minutes.
2. Remove the leaves from the cauliflower and trim the stem, so it sits flat.
3. Slice the cauliflower into 2.5 cm thick "steaks" from the centre, using a sharp knife. Be careful to keep the florets intact.
4. In a small bowl, combine olive oil, garlic powder, paprika, dried thyme, salt, and black pepper.
5. Brush both sides of each cauliflower steak with the oil and spice mixture.
6. Place the cauliflower steaks in the air fryer basket in a single layer. If necessary, cook them in batches to avoid overcrowding.
7. Air fry the cauliflower steaks at 200°C for 12-15 minutes, flipping halfway through, until they are tender and golden brown.
8. Remove the air-fried cauliflower steaks from the air fryer and transfer them to a serving plate.
9. Garnish with fresh herbs and serve with lemon wedges for added zest, if desired.

Green Beans with Garlic and Almonds

Prep Time: 10 minutes / Cook time: 10 minutes
Serves: 4

Ingredients:

• 500g green beans, trimmed
• 2 tablespoons olive oil
• 2 cloves garlic, minced
• 1/4 cup sliced almonds
• 1/2 teaspoon lemon zest
• Salt and black pepper, to taste
• Lemon wedges, for serving

Instructions:

1. Preheat the air fryer to 200°C for 5 minutes.
2. In a large bowl, toss the green beans with olive oil, minced garlic, sliced almonds, lemon zest, salt, and black pepper until well coated.
3. Place the seasoned green beans in the air fryer basket in a single layer. If necessary, cook them in batches to avoid overcrowding.
4. Air fry the green beans at 200°C for 8-10 minutes, shaking the basket or tossing the beans halfway through the cooking time.
5. Once the green beans are crisp-tender and lightly browned, remove them from the air fryer.
6. Transfer the air-fried green beans to a serving dish and squeeze fresh lemon juice over them.
7. Serve hot as a flavourful and nutritious side dish.

Broccoli Tenderstems with Lemon and Garlic

Prep Time: 10 minutes / Cook time: 10 minutes
Serves: 4

Ingredients:

• 500g broccoli tenderstems
• 2 tablespoons olive oil
• 2 cloves garlic, minced
• 1 teaspoon lemon zest
• Salt and black pepper, to taste

- Lemon wedges, for serving

Instructions:

1. Preheat the air fryer to 200°C for 5 minutes.
2. In a large bowl, toss the broccoli tenderstems with olive oil, minced garlic, lemon zest, salt, and black pepper until well coated.
3. Place the seasoned broccoli tenderstems in the air fryer basket in a single layer. If necessary, cook them in batches to avoid overcrowding.
4. Air fry the broccoli tenderstems at 200°C for 8-10 minutes, shaking the basket or tossing the tenderstems halfway through the cooking time.
5. Once the tenderstems are crisp-tender and lightly charred, remove them from the air fryer.
6. Transfer the air-fried broccoli tenderstems to a serving dish.
7. Serve hot with lemon wedges on the side for an extra burst of citrus flavour.

Air-Fried Corn "Ribs" with Smoky Seasoning

Prep Time: 15 minutes / Cook time: 15 minutes
Serves: 4

Ingredients:

- 4 ears of corn, husked
- 2 tablespoons olive oil
- 1 teaspoon smoked paprika
- 1/2 teaspoon garlic powder
- 1/2 teaspoon onion powder
- 1/4 teaspoon cumin
- 1/4 teaspoon salt
- 1/4 teaspoon black pepper
- Optional toppings: chopped fresh coriander, lime wedges

Instructions:

1. Preheat the air fryer to 200°C for 5 minutes.
2. Cut each corn ear into quarters to create corn "ribs."
3. In a small bowl, combine olive oil, smoked paprika, garlic powder, onion powder, cumin, salt, and black pepper.
4. Brush the corn "ribs" with the seasoned oil mixture, ensuring they are well coated.
5. Place the seasoned corn "ribs" in the air fryer basket in a single layer. If necessary, cook them in batches to avoid overcrowding.
6. Air fry the corn "ribs" at 200°C for 12-15 minutes, shaking the basket or turning the "ribs" halfway through the cooking time.
7. Once the corn "ribs" are golden brown and slightly charred, remove them from the air fryer.
8. Transfer the air-fried corn "ribs" to a serving dish.
9. Sprinkle with chopped fresh coriander and serve with lime wedges on the side for a fresh and zesty touch.

Aubergine Parmesan Rounds

Prep Time: 15 minutes / Cook time: 15 minutes
Serves: 4

Ingredients:

1 large aubergine, sliced into 1.5 cm rounds
- 100g breadcrumbs (preferably wholemeal)
- 25g grated Parmesan cheese
- 1 teaspoon dried oregano
- 1/2 teaspoon garlic powder
- 1/2 teaspoon salt
- 1/4 teaspoon black pepper
- 2 eggs, beaten
- 200g marinara sauce
- 100g shredded mozzarella cheese

Instructions:

1. Preheat the air fryer to 200°C for 5 minutes.
2. In a shallow dish, combine the breadcrumbs, grated Parmesan cheese, dried oregano, garlic powder, salt, and black pepper.
3. Dip each aubergine round into the beaten eggs, allowing any excess to drip off, and then coat it in the breadcrumb mixture. Press gently to adhere the breadcrumbs to the aubergine.
4. Place the breaded aubergine rounds in the air fryer basket in a single layer. If necessary, cook them in batches to avoid overcrowding.
5. Air fry the aubergine rounds at 200°C for 12-15 minutes, flipping them halfway through the cooking time for even browning.
6. Once the aubergine rounds are golden brown and crisp, remove them from the air fryer and place them on a paper towel-lined plate to absorb any excess oil.
7. Preheat the grill in your oven to high heat.
8. Arrange the air-fried aubergine rounds on a baking sheet lined with parchment paper. Top each round with a spoonful of marinara sauce and a sprinkle of shredded mozzarella cheese.
9. Place the baking sheet under the grill for 2-3 minutes, or until the cheese is melted and bubbly.
10. Remove from the oven and let the aubergine Parmesan rounds cool slightly before serving.

Air-Fried Stuffed Tomatoes

Prep Time: 15 minutes / Cook time: 15 minutes
Serves: 4

Ingredients:

- 4 large tomatoes
- 110 g cooked quinoa
- 1 small onion, finely chopped
- 1 pepper, finely chopped
- 2 cloves garlic, minced
- 55 g grated cheddar cheese

- 2 tablespoons chopped fresh basil
- 1 tablespoon olive oil
- 1/2 teaspoon dried oregano
- Salt and black pepper, to taste

Instructions:

1. Preheat the air fryer to 180°C for 5 minutes.
2. Cut off the tops of the tomatoes and scoop out the pulp and seeds with a spoon, leaving a hollow shell. Reserve the pulp for later use.
3. In a mixing bowl, combine the cooked quinoa, chopped onion, bell pepper, minced garlic, grated cheddar cheese, chopped fresh basil, olive oil, dried oregano, salt, and black pepper. Mix well to combine.
4. Stuff each hollowed tomato with the quinoa mixture, pressing it down gently.
5. Place the stuffed tomatoes in the air fryer basket. If necessary, cook them in batches to avoid overcrowding.
6. Air fry the stuffed tomatoes at 180°C for 12-15 minutes until the tomatoes are soft and the filling is heated through.
7. While the tomatoes are cooking, blend the reserved tomato pulp in a blender until smooth to create a tomato sauce.
8. Once the stuffed tomatoes are done, remove them from the air fryer and serve hot with a drizzle of the tomato sauce.

Tomato and Feta Stuffed Peppers

Prep Time: 15 minutes / Cook time: 15 minutes
Serves: 4

Ingredients:

- 4 peppers (any colour), halved and seeded
- 200g cherry tomatoes, halved
- 100g feta cheese, crumbled
- 2 tablespoons chopped fresh parsley
- 1 tablespoon olive oil
- 1 teaspoon dried oregano
- Salt and black pepper, to taste

Instructions:

1. Preheat the air fryer to 180°C for 5 minutes.
2. In a mixing bowl, combine the cherry tomatoes, crumbled feta cheese, chopped fresh parsley, olive oil, dried oregano, salt, and black pepper. Mix well to combine.
3. Stuff each pepper half with the tomato and feta mixture, pressing it down gently.
4. Place the stuffed pepper halves in the air fryer basket. If necessary, cook them in batches to avoid overcrowding.
5. Air fry the stuffed peppers at 180°C for 12-15 minutes until the peppers are tender and the filling is heated through.

6. Once the stuffed peppers are done, remove them from the air fryer and serve hot.

Loaded Potato Skins

Prep Time: 15 minutes / Cook time: 30 minutes
Serves: 4

Ingredients:

- 4 large baking potatoes
- 2 tablespoons olive oil
- Salt and black pepper, to taste
- 6 slices bacon, cooked and crumbled
- 100 g shredded cheddar cheese
- 30 g chopped green onions
- 6 0g sour cream
- Optional toppings: chopped tomatoes, sliced jalapenos, chopped fresh parsley

Instructions:

1. Preheat the air fryer to 200°C for 5 minutes.
2. Scrub the potatoes clean and pat them dry. Pierce the potatoes all over with a fork.
3. Rub the potatoes with olive oil and sprinkle them with salt and black pepper.
4. Place the potatoes in the air fryer basket and air fry them at 200°C for 30 minutes or until they are cooked through and the skin is crispy.
5. Once the potatoes are done, remove them from the air fryer and let them cool slightly.
6. Cut the potatoes in half lengthwise. Scoop out most of the flesh, leaving a thin layer attached to the skin.
7. Place the potato skins back in the air fryer basket, cut side up. Air fry them at 200°C for 5 minutes to crisp them up.
8. Fill each potato skin with crumbled bacon, shredded cheddar cheese, and chopped green onions.
9. Place the loaded potato skins back in the air fryer and air fry them at 200°C for an additional 3-5 minutes, or until the cheese is melted and bubbly.
10. Remove the potato skins from the air fryer and top them with sour cream and any optional toppings you desire, such as chopped tomatoes, sliced jalapenos, or chopped fresh parsley.

Cauliflower Cheese

Prep Time: 15 minutes / Cook time: 25 minutes
Serves: 4

Ingredients:

- 1 medium head of cauliflower, cut into florets
- 25g unsalted butter
- 25g plain flour
- 240ml milk
- 100g grated cheddar cheese
- 1/4 teaspoon garlic powder
- 1/4 teaspoon mustard powder

- Salt and black pepper, to taste
- Chopped fresh parsley, for garnish (optional)

Instructions:

1. Preheat the air fryer to 180°Cfor 5 minutes.
2. Place the cauliflower florets in a steamer basket and steam them for 5-7 minutes until they are slightly tender. Set aside.
3. In a small saucepan, melt the butter over medium heat. Add the flour and whisk continuously for 1-2 minutes until the mixture becomes smooth and bubbly.
4. Gradually pour in the milk while whisking constantly to prevent lumps from forming. Continue cooking and whisking until the mixture thickens.
5. Remove the saucepan from heat and stir in the grated cheddar cheese, garlic powder, mustard powder, salt, and black pepper. Mix until the cheese has melted and the sauce is smooth and creamy.
6. Place the steamed cauliflower florets in a bowl that fits in the air fryer basket and pour the cheese sauce over them, ensuring they are well coated.
7. Air fry the cauliflower at 180°C for 15-20 minutes until the cheese is golden and bubbly, and the cauliflower is tender.
8. Once the cauliflower cheese is done, remove it from the air fryer and let it cool slightly.
9. Garnish with chopped fresh parsley, if desired, and serve hot as a tasty side dish.

Spinach and Feta Stuffed Mushrooms

Prep Time: 15 minutes / Cook time: 12 minutes
Serves: 4

Ingredients:

- 8 large button mushrooms
- 70 g fresh spinach, chopped
- 100g feta cheese, crumbled
- 30 g finely chopped onion
- 1 clove garlic, minced
- 1 tablespoon olive oil
- Salt and black pepper, to taste

Instructions:

1. Preheat the air fryer to 180°C for 5 minutes.
2. Remove the stems from the mushrooms and set them aside. Place the mushroom caps in the air fryer basket.
3. In a frying pan, heat the olive oil over medium heat. Add the chopped mushroom stems, onion, and garlic. Sauté for 3-4 minutes until the vegetables are softened.
4. Add the chopped spinach to the frying pan and cook for another 2-3 minutes until wilted.
5. Remove the frying pan from the heat and let the mixture cool slightly. Stir in the crumbled feta cheese and season with salt and black pepper.

6. Spoon the spinach and feta mixture into each mushroom cap, filling them generously.
7. Place the stuffed mushrooms in the air fryer basket. If necessary, cook them in batches to avoid overcrowding.
8. Air fry the stuffed mushrooms at 180°C for 10-12 minutes until the mushrooms are tender and the filling is heated through.
9. Once the stuffed mushrooms are done, remove them from the air fryer and let them cool slightly.

Sweet Potato and Spinach Quesadillas

Prep Time: 15 minutes / Cook time: 10 minutes
Serves:2

Ingredients:

- 2 medium sweet potatoes, peeled and cubed
- 2 tablespoons olive oil, divided
- 1 teaspoon ground cumin
- 1/2 teaspoon paprika
- Salt and black pepper, to taste
- 2 large whole wheat tortillas
- 30 g fresh spinach leaves
- 60 g shredded mozzarella cheese
- 30 g crumbled feta cheese
- Optional toppings: Greek yogurt, chopped fresh coriander

Instructions:

1. Preheat the air fryer to 200°C for 5 minutes.
2. In a bowl, toss the sweet potato cubes with 1 tablespoon of olive oil, ground cumin, paprika, salt, and black pepper until evenly coated.
3. Place the seasoned sweet potatoes in the air fryer basket and air fry them at 200°C for 10 minutes or until they are tender and lightly browned. Set aside.
4. Lay one tortilla on a flat surface. Arrange half of the spinach leaves evenly over one half of the tortilla.
5. Spread half of the air-fried sweet potatoes over the spinach leaves.
6. Sprinkle half of the shredded mozzarella and crumbled feta cheese over the sweet potatoes.
7. Fold the empty half of the tortilla over the filling to create a half-moon shape.
8. Repeat steps 4-7 with the remaining tortilla and ingredients.
9. Brush the outer surface of each quesadilla with the remaining tablespoon of olive oil.
10. Place the quesadillas in the air fryer basket and air fry them at 200°C for 5 minutes or until the cheese is melted and the tortillas are crispy and golden.
11. Remove the quesadillas from the air fryer and let them cool slightly.
12. Slice the quesadillas into wedges and serve them with optional toppings such as Greek yogurt and chopped

fresh coriander.

Spicy Chickpea Snacks

Prep Time: 10 minutes / Cook time: 15 minutes
Serves: 4

Ingredients:

- 2 cans (400g each) chickpeas, drained and rinsed
- 2 tablespoons olive oil
- 1 teaspoon smoked paprika
- 1/2 teaspoon ground cumin
- 1/2 teaspoon garlic powder
- 1/4 teaspoon cayenne pepper (adjust to taste)
- Salt, to taste
- Fresh lemon wedges, for serving

Instructions:

1. Preheat the air fryer to 200°C for 5 minutes.
2. Place the drained and rinsed chickpeas on a clean kitchen towel and pat them dry to remove any excess moisture.
3. In a bowl, combine the olive oil, smoked paprika, ground cumin, garlic powder, cayenne pepper, and salt. Mix well.
4. Add the dried chickpeas to the spice mixture and toss until they are coated evenly.
5. Place the seasoned chickpeas in the air fryer basket.
6. Air fry the chickpeas at 200°C for 15 minutes, shaking the basket halfway through to ensure even cooking.
7. Once the chickpeas are crispy and golden brown, remove them from the air fryer and let them cool slightly.
8. Serve the air-fried spicy chickpea snacks as a healthy and flavourful appetiser or snack.
9. Squeeze fresh lemon juice over the chickpeas for an extra tangy kick, if desired.

Air Fryer Baked Potato Wedges with Herbs

Prep Time: 10 minutes / Cook time: 20-25 minutes
Serves: 4

Ingredients:

- 4 large potatoes, peeled and cut into wedges
- 2 tbsp olive oil
- 1 tsp dried oregano
- 1 tsp dried thyme
- Salt and pepper, to taste
- 2 tbsp grated parmesan cheese, for garnish (optional)

Instructions:

1. Preheat the air fryer to 400°F (200°C).
2. In a large bowl, mix together the potato wedges, olive oil, dried oregano, dried thyme, salt, and pepper.
3. Place the potato mixture in the air fryer basket in a single layer, making sure not to overcrowd. Cook for 20-25 minutes, or until the potatoes are tender and crispy.
4. Remove the potatoes from the air fryer and sprinkle with grated parmesan cheese, if desired.
5. Serve hot as a side dish or topped with additional seasonings and toppings of your choice. Enjoy!

Fig, Chickpea, and Rocket Salad

Prep Time: 15 minutes / Cook time: 20 minutes
Serves: 4

Ingredients

- 8 fresh figs, halved
- 250 g cooked chickpeas
- 1 teaspoon crushed roasted cumin seeds
- 4 tablespoons balsamic vinegar
- 2 tablespoons extra-virgin olive oil, plus more for greasing
- Salt and ground black pepper, to taste
- 40 g rocket, washed and dried

Instructions

1. Preheat the air fryer to 192°C.
2. Cover the air fryer basket with aluminium foil and grease lightly with oil. Put the figs in the air fryer basket and air fry for 10 minutes.
3. In a bowl, combine the chickpeas and cumin seeds.
4. Remove the air fried figs from the air fryer and replace with the chickpeas. Air fry for 10 minutes. Leave to cool.
5. In the meantime, prepare the dressing. Mix the balsamic vinegar, olive oil, salt and pepper.
6. In a salad bowl, combine the rocket with the cooled figs and chickpeas.
7. Toss with the sauce and serve.

Chapter 7 Family Favourites

Air-Fried Chicken Drumsticks

Prep Time: 10 minutes / Cook time: 25 minutes
Serves: 4

Ingredients:

- 8 chicken drumsticks
- 2 tablespoons olive oil
- 1 teaspoon smoked paprika
- 1 teaspoon dried thyme
- 1/2 teaspoon garlic powder
- 1/2 teaspoon onion powder
- Salt and black pepper, to taste

Instructions:

1. Preheat the air fryer to 200°C for 5 minutes.
2. In a bowl, combine olive oil, smoked paprika, dried thyme, garlic powder, onion powder, salt, and black pepper.
3. Pat the chicken drumsticks dry with a paper towel and coat them with the spice mixture.
4. Place the drumsticks in the air fryer basket, making sure they are not overcrowded.
5. Air fry the chicken drumsticks at 200°C for 20-25 minutes, flipping them halfway through, until they are golden brown and cooked through.
6. Remove the drumsticks from the air fryer and let them rest for a few minutes before serving.

Fish and Chips

Prep Time: 15 minutes / Cook time: 20 minutes
Serves: 4

Ingredients:

- 4 white fish fillets (such as cod or haddock)
- 100g plain flour
- 2 eggs, beaten
- 100g breadcrumbs
- 1 teaspoon paprika
- Salt and black pepper, to taste
- Olive oil cooking spray
- 800g potatoes, cut into chips
- Salt, to taste

Instructions:

1. Preheat the air fryer to 200°C for 5 minutes.
2. Pat the fish fillets dry with a paper towel and season them with salt and black pepper.
3. Set up a dredging station with three shallow bowls. Place the flour in one bowl, beaten eggs in another bowl, and breadcrumbs mixed with paprika in the third bowl.
4. Dip each fish fillet into the flour, shaking off any excess. Then dip it into the beaten eggs, followed by the breadcrumb mixture, pressing gently to adhere.
5. Spray the air fryer basket with olive oil cooking spray. Place the breaded fish fillets in the basket, ensuring they are not overlapping.
6. In a separate bowl, toss the potato chips with olive oil and salt.
7. Place the potato chips in the air fryer basket alongside the fish fillets.
8. Air fry the fish and chips at 200°C for 15-20 minutes, flipping the fish fillets and shaking the basket halfway through, until the fish is golden and the chips are crispy.
9. Serve the air-fried fish and chips with lemon wedges and your choice of condiments.

Apple Pie Pockets

Prep Time: 20 minutes / Cook time: 12 minutes
Makes: 4 apple pie pockets

Ingredients:

- 2 apples, peeled, cored, and diced
- 2 tablespoons granulated sugar
- 1/2 teaspoon ground cinnamon
- 1/4 teaspoon ground nutmeg
- 1 tablespoon lemon juice
- 4 sheets ready-made puff pastry
- 1 egg, beaten (for egg wash)
- Icing sugar, for dusting (optional)

Instructions:

1. Preheat the air fryer to 180°C for 5 minutes.
2. In a bowl,l, combine the diced apples, granulated sugar, ground cinnamon, ground nutmeg, and lemon juice. Mix well to coat the apples in the sugar and spices.
3. Roll out the puff pastry sheets and cut them into squares or rectangles, depending on the desired size of your apple pie pockets.
4. Place a spoonful of the apple mixture onto one-half of each pastry square. Fold the other half over to create a pocket and seal the edges by pressing them together with a fork.
5. Brush the tops of the pastry pockets with beaten egg wash for a golden finish.
6. Place the apple pie pockets in the air fryer basket, ensuring they are not touching each other.
7. Air fry the apple pie pockets at 180°C for 10-12

minutes, or until the pastry is crisp and golden.

8. Once cooked, remove the apple pie pockets from the air fryer and allow them to cool slightly.

9. Optionally, dust the pockets with icing sugar for a touch of sweetness before serving.

10. Serve the air-fried apple pie pockets warm as a delightful dessert or a sweet treat.

Chicken Nuggets

Prep Time: 15 minutes / Cook time: 12 minutes
Serves: 4

Ingredients:

- 500g boneless, skinless chicken breasts, cut into bite-sized pieces
- 100g plain flour
- 2 large eggs, beaten
- 100g breadcrumbs
- 1 teaspoon paprika
- 1/2 teaspoon garlic powder
- 1/2 teaspoon onion powder
- 1/2 teaspoon dried mixed herbs
- Salt and black pepper, to taste
- Olive oil cooking spray

Instructions:

1. Preheat the air fryer to 200°C for 5 minutes.

2. In separate bowls, place the flour, beaten eggs, and breadcrumbs.

3. Add paprika, garlic powder, onion powder, dried mixed herbs, salt, and black pepper to the breadcrumbs. Mix well to combine the spices.

4. Dip each chicken piece into the flour, then into the beaten eggs, and finally coat it with the seasoned breadcrumbs, pressing gently to adhere.

5. Spray the air fryer basket with olive oil cooking spray. Place the coated chicken nuggets in a single layer in the basket, ensuring they are not overlapping.

6. Lightly spray the tops of the chicken nuggets with olive oil cooking spray.

7. Air fry the chicken nuggets at 200°C for 10-12 minutes, flipping them halfway through, until they are golden brown and cooked through.

8. Once cooked, remove the chicken nuggets from the air fryer and let them rest for a few minutes before serving.

Vegetable Spring Rolls

Prep Time: 30 minutes / Cook time: 12 minutes
Serves: 4

Ingredients:

- 8 spring roll wrappers
- 200g mixed vegetables (such as shredded cabbage, grated carrots, sliced peppers, and bean sprouts)
- 1 tablespoon soy sauce
- 1 teaspoon sesame oil
- 1 teaspoon grated ginger
- 1 clove garlic, minced
- 1 tablespoon cornflour mixed with 2 tablespoons water (for sealing)
- Olive oil cooking spray
- Sweet chili sauce, for dipping

Instructions:

1. Preheat the air fryer to 180°C for 5 minutes.

2. In a bowl, combine the mixed vegetables, soy sauce, sesame oil, grated ginger, and minced garlic. Mix well to coat the vegetables in the seasoning.

3. Place a spring roll wrapper on a clean surface and spoon a portion of the vegetable mixture onto the centre of the wrapper.

4. Fold the sides of the wrapper over the filling, then roll it tightly from the bottom to the top, sealing the edges with the cornflour-water mixture.

5. Repeat the process with the remaining spring roll wrappers and vegetable filling.

6. Lightly spray the air fryer basket with olive oil cooking spray. Place the spring rolls in the basket, ensuring they are not touching each other.

7. Lightly spray the tops of the spring rolls with olive oil cooking spray.

8. Air fry the spring rolls at 180°C for 10-12 minutes, flipping them halfway through, until they are golden and crispy.

9. Once cooked, remove the spring rolls from the air fryer and let them cool slightly.

10. Serve the air-fried vegetable spring rolls with sweet chili sauce for dipping and enjoy!

Air-Fried Chicken Parmesan

Prep Time: 15 minutes / Cook time: 20 minutes
Serves: 4

Ingredients:

- 4 boneless, skinless chicken breasts
- 100g plain flour
- 2 large eggs, beaten
- 100g breadcrumbs
- 50g grated Parmesan cheese
- 1 teaspoon dried oregano
- 1/2 teaspoon garlic powder
- 1/2 teaspoon onion powder
- Salt and black pepper, to taste
- 400g passata or tomato sauce
- 1 teaspoon dried basil
- 1 teaspoon dried thyme
- 1/2 teaspoon sugar
- 200g mozzarella cheese, sliced
- Fresh basil leaves, for garnish (optional)

Instructions:

1. Preheat the air fryer to 200°C for 5 minutes.
2. Place the chicken breasts between two sheets of plastic wrap and pound them to an even thickness.
3. In separate bowls, place the flour, beaten eggs, and breadcrumbs.
4. Add grated Parmesan cheese, dried oregano, garlic powder, onion powder, salt, and black pepper to the breadcrumbs. Mix well to combine the seasonings.
5. Dip each chicken breast into the flour, then into the beaten eggs, and finally coat it with the seasoned breadcrumbs, pressing gently to adhere.
6. Spray the air fryer basket with olive oil cooking spray. Place the coated chicken breasts in the basket, ensuring they are not overlapping.
7. Lightly spray the tops of the chicken breasts with olive oil cooking spray.
8. Air fry the chicken breasts at 200°C for 15 minutes, flipping them halfway through, until they are golden brown and cooked through.
9. In a saucepan, heat the passata or tomato sauce over medium heat. Add dried basil, dried thyme, sugar, salt, and black pepper to taste. Simmer for a few minutes until the sauce is heated through.
10. Once cooked, remove the chicken breasts from the air fryer and spoon the tomato sauce over each breast.
11. Place slices of mozzarella cheese on top of the tomato sauce.
12. Return the chicken breasts to the air fryer and cook for an additional 5 minutes, or until the cheese is melted and bubbly.
13. Garnish with fresh basil leaves, if desired, and serve the air-fried chicken Parmesan with pasta or a side salad.

Vegetable Samosas

Prep Time: 30 minutes / Cook time: 15 minutes
Serves: 4

Ingredients:

- 8 samosa pastry sheets (available at most supermarkets)
- 1 large potato, boiled and mashed
- 100g green peas, boiled
- 1 small carrot, grated
- 1 small onion, finely chopped
- 1 teaspoon cumin seeds
- 1 teaspoon ground coriander
- 1/2 teaspoon turmeric powder
- 1/2 teaspoon garam masala
- 1/2 teaspoon red chili powder (optional)
- Salt, to taste
- Vegetable oil, for brushing

Instructions:

1. Preheat the air fryer to 180°C for 5 minutes.
2. In a pan, heat a little vegetable oil and add the cumin seeds. Sauté until they start to crackle.
3. Add the chopped onion and cook until it becomes translucent.
4. Add the grated carrot and boiled green peas. Cook for a couple of minutes.
5. Add the mashed potato, ground coriander, turmeric powder, garam masala, red chili powder (if using), and salt. Mix well to combine all the ingredients and cook for another 2-3 minutes.
6. Remove the mixture from heat and let it cool.
7. Take a samosa pastry sheet and fold it into a cone shape, sealing the edges with water or a flour-water paste.
8. Fill the cone with the vegetable mixture and seal the top by folding it over.
9. Repeat the process with the remaining pastry sheets and vegetable mixture.
10. Lightly brush the samosas with vegetable oil.
11. Place the samosas in the air fryer basket, ensuring they are not touching each other.
12. Air fry the samosas at 180°C for 12-15 minutes, until they turn golden brown and crispy.
13. Once cooked, remove the samosas from the air fryer and let them cool for a few minutes before serving.
14. Serve the air-fried vegetable samosas with mint chutney or your favourite dipping sauce.

Chicken Satay Skewers

Prep Time: 20 minutes / Cook time: 12 minutes
Serves: 4

Ingredients:

- 4 chicken breasts, cut into strips
- 2 tablespoons soy sauce
- 2 tablespoons peanut butter
- 1 tablespoon honey
- 1 tablespoon lime juice
- 1 clove garlic, minced
- 1 teaspoon grated ginger
- 1/2 teaspoon turmeric powder
- 1/2 teaspoon cumin powder
- 1/4 teaspoon chili powder (optional)
- Salt, to taste
- Bamboo skewers, soaked in water for 30 minutes

Instructions:

1. Preheat the air fryer to 180°C for 5 minutes.
2. In a bowl, whisk together the soy sauce, peanut butter, honey, lime juice, minced garlic, grated ginger, turmeric powder, cumin powder, chili powder (if using), and salt.
3. Add the chicken strips to the bowl and marinate for at

least 10 minutes.

4. Thread the marinated chicken strips onto the soaked bamboo skewers.

5. Lightly spray the air fryer basket with cooking oil.

6. Place the chicken skewers in the air fryer, ensuring they are not touching each other.

7. Air fry the chicken satay skewers at 180°C for 10-12 minutes, flipping them halfway through, until they are cooked through and nicely charred.

8. Once cooked, remove the chicken satay skewers from the air fryer and let them rest for a few minutes before serving.

9. Serve the air-fried chicken satay skewers with peanut sauce or a side of steamed rice.

Scotch Eggs

Prep Time: 20 minutes / Cook time: 15 minutes
Serves: 4

Ingredients:

- 4 large eggs
- 400g sausage meat
- 50g breadcrumbs
- 1 tablespoon dried parsley
- 1/2 teaspoon dried thyme
- 1/2 teaspoon dried sage
- Salt and black pepper, to taste
- 50g plain flour
- 2 large eggs, beaten
- Olive oil cooking spray

Instructions:

1. Preheat the air fryer to 180°C for 5 minutes.

2. Place the eggs in a saucepan and cover them with cold water. Bring the water to a boil, then reduce the heat and simmer for 4-5 minutes for a soft-boiled texture. Drain the hot water and transfer the eggs to a bowl of cold water to cool.

3. Once the eggs are cool, carefully peel off the shells and set them aside.

4. In a mixing bowl, combine the sausage meat, breadcrumbs, dried parsley, dried thyme, dried sage, salt, and black pepper. Mix well to combine all the ingredients.

5. Divide the sausage mixture into 4 equal portions. Flatten each portion in your hand and place a boiled egg in the centre. Wrap the sausage meat around the egg, ensuring it is completely covered.

6. Set up a breading station with three shallow bowls: one with flour, one with beaten eggs, and one with breadcrumbs.

7. Roll each sausage-wrapped egg in the flour, then dip it into the beaten eggs, and finally coat it with breadcrumbs, pressing gently to adhere.

8. Lightly spray the air fryer basket with olive oil

cooking spray. Place the coated scotch eggs in the basket, ensuring they are not touching each other.

9. Lightly spray the tops of the scotch eggs with olive oil cooking spray.

10. Air fry the scotch eggs at 180°C for 12-15 minutes, until they are golden brown and cooked through.

11. Once cooked, remove the scotch eggs from the air fryer and let them cool for a few minutes before serving.

Teriyaki Salmon

Prep Time: 10 minutes / Cook time: 12 minutes
Serves: 4

Ingredients:

- 4 salmon fillets
- 4 tablespoons soy sauce
- 2 tablespoons honey
- 1 tablespoon rice vinegar
- 1 tablespoon sesame oil
- 1 clove garlic, minced
- 1 teaspoon grated ginger
- 1 tablespoon cornflour
- 2 tablespoons water
- Sesame seeds, for garnish
- Spring onions, sliced, for garnish

Instructions:

1. Preheat the air fryer to 200°C for 5 minutes.

2. In a small bowl, whisk together the soy sauce, honey, rice vinegar, sesame oil, minced garlic, and grated ginger to make the teriyaki sauce.

3. Place the salmon fillets in a shallow dish and pour half of the teriyaki sauce over them, reserving the remaining sauce for later. Allow the salmon to marinate for about 5 minutes.

4. Place the marinated salmon fillets in the air fryer basket, leaving space between them for air circulation.

5. Air fry the salmon at 200°C for 10-12 minutes, or until cooked to your desired level of doneness.

6. In the meantime, in a small bowl, mix the cornflour and water together to make a slurry.

7. Heat the reserved teriyaki sauce in a small saucepan over medium heat. Once it begins to simmer, stir in the cornflour slurry. Cook, stirring constantly, until the sauce thickens to your desired consistency.

8. Remove the cooked salmon from the air fryer and drizzle with the thickened teriyaki sauce.

9. Sprinkle sesame seeds and sliced spring onions on top for garnish.

Mediterranean Stuffed Peppers

Prep Time: 20 minutes / Cook time: 20 minutes
Serves: 4

Ingredients:

- 4 peppers (any colour)
- 200g cooked quinoa
- 200g canned chickpeas, rinsed and drained
- 100g feta cheese, crumbled
- 50g sun-dried tomatoes, chopped
- 50g black olives, sliced
- 1 small red onion, finely chopped
- 2 tablespoons chopped fresh parsley
- 1 tablespoon olive oil
- 1 teaspoon dried oregano
- Salt and black pepper, to taste

Instructions:

1. Preheat the air fryer to 180°C for 5 minutes.
2. Cut the tops off the peppers and remove the seeds and membranes from the inside. Rinse the peppers under cold water.
3. In a large mixing bowl, combine the cooked quinoa, chickpeas, feta cheese, sun-dried tomatoes, black olives, red onion, chopped parsley, olive oil, dried oregano, salt, and black pepper. Mix well to combine all the ingredients.
4. Stuff each pepper with the quinoa mixture, packing it tightly.
5. Place the stuffed bell peppers in the air fryer basket, standing upright and ensuring they are stable and not leaning over.
6. Air fry the stuffed peppers at 180°C for 18-20 minutes, or until the peppers are tender and the filling is heated through.
7. Once cooked, carefully remove the stuffed peppers from the air fryer and let them cool for a few minutes before serving.

Chicken and Vegetable Skewers

Prep Time: 20 minutes / Cook time: 15 minutes
Serves: 4

Ingredients:

- 4 boneless, skinless chicken breasts, cut into chunks
- 1 red pepper, cut into chunks
- 1 green pepper, cut into chunks
- 1 red onion, cut into chunks
- 200g cherry tomatoes
- 2 tablespoons olive oil
- 2 tablespoons lemon juice
- 2 cloves garlic, minced
- 1 teaspoon dried oregano
- 1 teaspoon dried basil
- Salt and black pepper, to taste

- Wooden skewers, soaked in water for 30 minutes

Instructions:

1. Preheat the air fryer to 200°C for 5 minutes.
2. In a bowl, combine the olive oil, lemon juice, minced garlic, dried oregano, dried basil, salt, and black pepper. Mix well to make the marinade.
3. Thread the chicken chunks, peppers, red onion, and cherry tomatoes onto the soaked wooden skewers, alternating the ingredients.
4. Place the skewers in a shallow dish and brush them generously with the marinade, making sure to coat all sides.
5. Place the chicken and vegetable skewers in the air fryer basket, leaving some space between them for even cooking.
6. Air fry the skewers at 200°C for 12-15 minutes, or until the chicken is cooked through and the vegetables are tender, turning the skewers halfway through the cooking time.
7. Once cooked, remove the skewers from the air fryer and let them cool for a few minutes before serving.

Lemon Herb Chicken Thighs

Prep Time: 10 minutes / Cook time: 20 minutes
Serves: 4

Ingredients:

- 8 chicken thighs, bone-in and skin-on
- 2 tablespoons olive oil
- Juice of 1 lemon
- Zest of 1 lemon
- 2 cloves garlic, minced
- 1 tablespoon chopped fresh thyme
- 1 tablespoon chopped fresh rosemary
- 1 teaspoon dried oregano
- Salt and black pepper, to taste
- Lemon wedges, for serving
- Chopped fresh parsley, for garnish

Instructions:

1. Preheat the air fryer to 200°C for 5 minutes.
2. In a bowl, whisk together the olive oil, lemon juice, lemon zest, minced garlic, chopped thyme, chopped rosemary, dried oregano, salt, and black pepper to make the marinade.
3. Pat dry the chicken thighs with paper towels and place them in a shallow dish. Pour the marinade over the chicken thighs, making sure they are well coated. Allow them to marinate for about 10 minutes.
4. Place the marinated chicken thighs in the air fryer basket, skin-side down. Make sure they are not touching each other to ensure even cooking.
5. Air fry the chicken thighs at 200°C for 10 minutes. Then, flip the chicken thighs and continue air frying for another 10 minutes, or until the chicken is cooked

through and the skin is crispy and golden brown.

6. Once cooked, remove the chicken thighs from the air fryer and let them rest for a few minutes.

7. Serve the air-fried lemon herb chicken thighs with lemon wedges on the side for an extra zesty touch. Garnish with chopped fresh parsley.

Sticky Sesame Chicken Wings

Prep Time: 10 minutes / Cook time: 20 minutes
Serves: 4

Ingredients:

- 1 kg chicken wings
- 3 tablespoons soy sauce
- 3 tablespoons honey
- 2 tablespoons tomato ketchup
- 2 tablespoons brown sugar
- 2 tablespoons rice vinegar
- 1 tablespoon sesame oil
- 2 cloves garlic, minced
- 1 teaspoon grated ginger
- 1 tablespoon cornflour
- 2 tablespoons water
- Sesame seeds, for garnish
- Sliced spring onions, for garnish

Instructions:

1. Preheat the air fryer to 200°C for 5 minutes.

2. In a bowl, whisk together the soy sauce, honey, tomato ketchup, brown sugar, rice vinegar, sesame oil, minced garlic, and grated ginger to make the sticky sauce.

3. Pat dry the chicken wings with paper towels and place them in a large bowl. Pour half of the sticky sauce over the chicken wings, reserving the remaining sauce for later. Toss the chicken wings to coat them evenly.

4. Place the chicken wings in the air fryer basket, leaving space between them for proper air circulation.

5. Air fry the chicken wings at 200°C for 10 minutes. Then, flip the wings and continue air frying for another 10 minutes, or until they are cooked through and crispy.

6. While the chicken wings are cooking, heat the reserved sticky sauce in a small saucepan over medium heat until it simmers.

7. In a separate small bowl, mix the cornflour and water together to make a slurry. Add the slurry to the simmering sauce and cook, stirring constantly, until the sauce thickens.

8. Once the chicken wings are cooked, remove them from the air fryer and let them rest for a few minutes.

9. Drizzle the thickened sticky sauce over the chicken wings, ensuring they are evenly coated. Sprinkle sesame seeds and sliced spring onions on top for garnish.

Falafel with Tzatziki Sauce

Prep Time: 15 minutes / Cook time: 15 minutes
Serves: 4

Ingredients:

- For the falafel:
- 400g canned chickpeas, drained and rinsed
- 1 small onion, roughly chopped
- 2 cloves garlic, minced
- 3 tablespoons fresh parsley, chopped
- 3 tablespoons fresh coriander, chopped
- 1 teaspoon ground cumin
- 1 teaspoon ground coriander
- 1/2 teaspoon salt
- 1/4 teaspoon black pepper
- 2 tablespoons plain flour
- 2 tablespoons olive oil
- For the tzatziki sauce:
- 150g Greek yogurt
- 1/2 cucumber, grated and squeezed to remove excess moisture
- 1 clove garlic, minced
- 1 tablespoon fresh dill, chopped
- 1 tablespoon fresh lemon juice
- Salt and black pepper, to taste

Instructions:

1. Preheat the air fryer to 200°C for 5 minutes.

2. In a food processor, combine the chickpeas, chopped onion, minced garlic, fresh parsley, fresh coriander, ground cumin, ground coriander, salt, black pepper, and plain flour. Pulse until the mixture comes together but is still slightly coarse.

3. Shape the falafel mixture into small balls or patties, about 2-3cm in diameter.

4. Brush the falafel balls or patties with olive oil, making sure to coat all sides.

5. Place the falafel in the air fryer basket, leaving space between them for even cooking.

6. Air fry the falafel at 200°C for 12-15 minutes, or until they are crispy and golden brown, turning them halfway through the cooking time.

7. While the falafel are cooking, prepare the tzatziki sauce. In a bowl, mix together the Greek yogurt, grated cucumber, minced garlic, chopped fresh dill, fresh lemon juice, salt, and black pepper. Stir well to combine.

8. Once the falafel are cooked, remove them from the air fryer and let them cool for a few minutes.

Coconut prawn with Mango Salsa

Prep Time: 20 minutes/Cook time: 10 minutes
Serves: 4

Ingredients:

- For the coconut prawn:
- 500g large prawn, peeled and deveined
- 100g plain flour
- 2 large eggs, beaten
- 100g desiccated coconut
- 1 teaspoon paprika
- 1/2 teaspoon garlic powder
- 1/2 teaspoon salt
- 1/4 teaspoon black pepper

For the mango salsa:

- 1 ripe mango, peeled and diced
- 1/2 red pepper, diced
- 1/4 red onion, finely chopped
- Juice of 1 lime
- 2 tablespoons chopped fresh coriander
- Salt and black pepper, to taste

Instructions:

1. Preheat the air fryer to 200°C for 5 minutes.
2. In three separate bowls, set up a breading station. Place the flour in one bowl, beaten eggs in another bowl, and a mixture of desiccated coconut, paprika, garlic powder, salt, and black pepper in the third bowl.
3. Dip each prawn into the flour, shaking off any excess. Then dip it into the beaten eggs, allowing any excess to drip off. Finally, coat the prawn in the coconut mixture, pressing gently to adhere. Repeat with the remaining prawn.
4. Place the coated prawn in the air fryer basket, making sure they are not touching each other.
5. Air fry the coconut prawn at 200°C for 8-10 minutes, or until they are golden brown and crispy, flipping them halfway through the cooking time.
6. While the prawn are cooking, prepare the mango salsa. In a bowl, combine the diced mango, diced red bell pepper, finely chopped red onion, lime juice, chopped fresh coriander, salt, and black pepper. Mix well to combine.
7. Once the coconut prawn are cooked, remove them from the air fryer and let them cool for a few minutes.
8. Serve the air-fried coconut prawn with the refreshing mango salsa on the side.

Honey Mustard Chicken Thighs

Prep Time: 10 minutes / Cook time: 20 minutes
Serves: 4

Ingredients:

- 8 bone-in, skin-on chicken thighs
- 3 tablespoons Dijon mustard
- 2 tablespoons honey
- 2 tablespoons olive oil
- 2 cloves garlic, minced
- 1 teaspoon dried thyme
- 1/2 teaspoon paprika
- Salt and black pepper, to taste
- Fresh parsley, for garnish

Instructions:

1. Preheat the air fryer to 200°C for 5 minutes.
2. In a small bowl, whisk together the Dijon mustard, honey, olive oil, minced garlic, dried thyme, paprika, salt, and black pepper.
3. Pat the chicken thighs dry with paper towels and place them in a large mixing bowl.
4. Pour the honey mustard mixture over the chicken thighs and toss until they are well coated.
5. Place the chicken thighs in the air fryer basket, skin side down, leaving space between them for even cooking.
6. Air fry the chicken thighs at 200°C for 10 minutes. Then flip the chicken thighs and continue air frying for another 10 minutes, or until the chicken is cooked through and the skin is crispy and golden brown.
7. Once the chicken thighs are cooked, remove them from the air fryer and let them rest for a few minutes.
8. Garnish with fresh parsley and serve the air-fried honey mustard chicken thighs with your choice of sides, such as roasted vegetables, mashed potatoes, or a fresh salad.

Vegetable Frittata

Prep Time: 10 minutes / Cook time: 20 minutes
Serves: 4

Ingredients:

- 8 large eggs
- 100g grated cheddar cheese
- 1 small onion, diced
- 1 red pepper, diced
- 1 courgette, diced
- 100g cherry tomatoes, halved
- 2 tablespoons chopped fresh parsley
- 1 tablespoon olive oil
- Salt and black pepper, to taste

Instructions:

1. Preheat the air fryer to 180°C for 5 minutes.
2. In a large bowl, whisk together the eggs, grated

cheddar cheese, chopped fresh parsley, salt, and black pepper. Set aside.

3. Heat the olive oil in a frying pan over medium heat. Add the diced onion, red bell pepper, and courgette. Sauté for 5-7 minutes, or until the vegetables are softened.
4. Transfer the sautéed vegetables to the egg mixture and stir to combine.
5. Pour the egg and vegetable mixture into a greased baking dish or into individual ramekins.
6. Place the baking dish or ramekins in the air fryer basket.
7. Air fry the vegetable frittata at 180°C for 15-20 minutes, or until the eggs are set and the top is lightly golden.
8. Once the frittata is cooked, remove it from the air fryer and let it cool for a few minutes.
9. Cut the frittata into slices or serve it directly from the ramekins.

Honey Glazed Salmon

Prep Time: 10 minutes / Cook time: 12 minutes
Serves: 4

Ingredients:
- 4 salmon fillets (150g each), skin-on
- 2 tablespoons honey
- 2 tablespoons soy sauce
- 2 tablespoons Dijon mustard
- 1 tablespoon olive oil
- 1 teaspoon minced garlic
- 1/2 teaspoon ground black pepper
- Lemon wedges, for serving
- Fresh parsley, chopped, for garnish

Instructions:
1. Preheat the air fryer to 200°C for 5 minutes.
2. In a small bowl, whisk together the honey, soy sauce, Dijon mustard, olive oil, minced garlic, and ground black pepper.
3. Place the salmon fillets, skin-side down, in a shallow dish and pour the honey glaze mixture over them. Make sure the fillets are evenly coated.
4. Place the salmon fillets in the air fryer basket, leaving space between them for even cooking.
5. Air fry the salmon at 200°C for 10-12 minutes, or until the fish is cooked through and flakes easily with a fork. The cooking time may vary depending on the thickness of the fillets.
6. Once cooked, remove the salmon fillets from the air fryer and let them rest for a few minutes.
7. Serve the air-fried honey glazed salmon with lemon wedges on the side. Sprinkle with fresh chopped parsley for garnish.

Air-Fried Fish Fingers

Prep Time: 15 minutes / Cook time: 12 minutes
Serves: 4

Ingredients:
- 400g white fish fillets (such as cod or haddock), cut into finger-sized strips
- 100g plain flour
- 2 eggs, beaten
- 100g breadcrumbs (preferably panko breadcrumbs)
- 1 teaspoon paprika
- 1/2 teaspoon garlic powder
- 1/2 teaspoon dried parsley
- Salt and black pepper, to taste
- Lemon wedges, for serving
- Tartar sauce or ketchup, for dipping

Instructions:
1. Preheat the air fryer to 200°C for 5 minutes.
2. In a shallow dish, combine the breadcrumbs, paprika, garlic powder, dried parsley, salt, and black pepper. Mix well.
3. Set up a dredging station with three separate bowls: one with plain flour, one with beaten eggs, and one with the breadcrumb mixture.
4. Dip each fish finger into the flour, shaking off any excess. Then dip it into the beaten eggs, allowing any excess to drip off. Finally, coat it thoroughly with the breadcrumb mixture, pressing gently to adhere.
5. Place the coated fish fingers in a single layer in the air fryer basket, leaving space between them for even cooking.
6. Air fry the fish fingers at 200°C for 10-12 minutes, or until they are golden brown and crispy. Flip the fish fingers halfway through cooking for even browning.
7. Once cooked, remove the fish fingers from the air fryer and let them cool for a few minutes.
8. Serve the air-fried fish fingers with lemon wedges and your choice of dipping sauce, such as tartar sauce or ketchup.

Mini Cheese and Tomato Pizzas

Prep Time: 15 minutes / Cook time: 8 minutes
Serves: 4

Ingredients:
- 4 small wholemeal pitta breads
- 4 tablespoons tomato passata
- 100g grated mozzarella cheese
- 1 small tomato, sliced
- 1/2 teaspoon dried oregano
- Salt and black pepper, to taste
- Fresh basil leaves, for garnish (optional)

Instructions:
1. Preheat the air fryer to 180°C for 5 minutes.

2. Slice each pitta bread in half to create mini pizza bases.
3. Spread 1 tablespoon of tomato passata on each pitta bread half.
4. Sprinkle grated mozzarella cheese evenly over the tomato passata.
5. Arrange tomato slices on top of the cheese.
6. Sprinkle dried oregano, salt, and black pepper over the pizzas.
7. Place the pizzas in the air fryer basket, leaving space between them for even cooking.
8. Air fry the mini pizzas at 180°C for 6-8 minutes, or until the cheese is melted and bubbly and the pitta bread is crispy.
9. Once cooked, remove the mini pizzas from the air fryer and let them cool for a few minutes.
10. Garnish with fresh basil leaves, if desired.

Chicken Quesadillas

Prep Time: 15 minutes / Cook time: 10 minutes
Serves: 4

Ingredients:

- 2 boneless, skinless chicken breasts, cooked and shredded
- 4 large flour tortillas
- 100g grated cheddar cheese
- 1/2 red pepper, diced
- 1/2 green pepper, diced
- 1/2 small red onion, diced
- 1 teaspoon ground cumin
- 1 teaspoon paprika
- Salt and black pepper, to taste
- Sour cream and salsa, for serving

Instructions:

1. Preheat the air fryer to 180°C for 5 minutes.
2. In a mixing bowl, combine the shredded chicken, diced peppers, diced red onion, ground cumin, paprika, salt, and black pepper. Mix well to evenly coat the chicken with the spices and vegetables.
3. Lay one tortilla flat on a clean surface. Spread a layer of the chicken and vegetable mixture on half of the tortilla.
4. Sprinkle grated cheddar cheese over the chicken mixture.
5. Fold the empty half of the tortilla over the filling to create a half-moon shape.
6. Repeat the process with the remaining tortillas and filling.
7. Place the folded quesadillas in the air fryer basket, leaving space between them for even cooking.
8. Air fry the quesadillas at 180°C for 8-10 minutes, or until the tortillas are crispy and the cheese is melted.
9. Once cooked, remove the quesadillas from the air fryer and let them cool for a few minutes.

Chicken and Vegetable Nuggets

Prep Time: 20 minutes / Cook time: 12 minutes
Serves: 4

Ingredients:

- 500g boneless, skinless chicken breasts, cut into chunks
- 1 medium carrot, grated
- 1 small courgette, grated
- 1/2 red onion, finely chopped
- 1 garlic clove, minced
- 1 teaspoon dried mixed herbs
- 1/2 teaspoon paprika
- 1/4 teaspoon salt
- 1/4 teaspoon black pepper
- 60g breadcrumbs
- 2 tablespoons grated Parmesan cheese
- 2 tablespoons plain flour
- 2 eggs, beaten

Instructions:

1. Preheat the air fryer to 200°C for 5 minutes.
2. In a mixing bowl, combine the chicken chunks, grated carrot, grated courgette, finely chopped red onion, minced garlic, dried mixed herbs, paprika, salt, and black pepper. Mix well to combine.
3. In a separate bowl, combine the breadcrumbs and grated Parmesan cheese.
4. Place the plain flour and beaten eggs in separate bowls.
5. Take a small portion of the chicken and vegetable mixture and shape it into a nugget.
6. Dip the nugget into the flour, shaking off any excess.
7. Next, dip the nugget into the beaten eggs, allowing any excess to drip off.
8. Finally, coat the nugget in the breadcrumb and Parmesan mixture, pressing lightly to adhere the breadcrumbs.
9. Place the coated nuggets in the air fryer basket, leaving space between them for even cooking.
10. Air fry the nuggets at 200°C for 10-12 minutes, or until golden brown and cooked through, flipping them halfway through the cooking time for even browning.

Air-Fried Cheesy Meatballs

Prep Time: 15 minutes / Cook Time: 12 minutes
Serves: 4

Ingredients:

- 500g lean beef mince
- 1/2 small onion, finely chopped
- 1 garlic clove, minced
- 25 g breadcrumbs
- 25 g grated Cheddar cheese
- 1 tablespoon Worcestershire sauce

- 1 tablespoon tomato ketchup
- 1/2 teaspoon dried oregano
- 1/2 teaspoon dried parsley
- 1/4 teaspoon salt
- 1/4 teaspoon black pepper

Instructions:

1. Preheat the air fryer to 200°C for 5 minutes.
2. In a mixing bowl, combine the beef mince, finely chopped onion, minced garlic, breadcrumbs, grated Cheddar cheese, Worcestershire sauce, tomato ketchup, dried oregano, dried parsley, salt, and black pepper. Mix well to combine all the ingredients.
3. Shape the mixture into bite-sized meatballs, about 2.5 cm in diameter.
4. Place the meatballs in the air fryer basket, leaving space between them for even cooking.
5. Air fry the meatballs at 200°C for 10-12 minutes, or until cooked through and browned on the outside, shaking the basket or flipping the meatballs halfway through the cooking time for even browning.
6. Once cooked, remove the meatballs from the air fryer and let them cool for a few minutes before serving.

Mini Pizza Pockets

Prep Time: 20 minutes / Cook Time: 10 minutes
Serves: 4

Ingredients:

- 1 sheet ready-made puff pastry, thawed
- 120 g tomato sauce
- 120 g grated mozzarella cheese
- 55 g sliced pepperoni or cooked ham
- 30 g sliced black olives
- 1/4 teaspoon dried oregano
- 1/4 teaspoon garlic powder
- 1/4 teaspoon onion powder
- 1 tablespoon olive oil, for brushing
- Fresh basil leaves, for garnish (optional)

Instructions:

1. Preheat the air fryer to 180°C for 5 minutes.
2. Roll out the puff pastry sheet on a lightly floured surface. Cut it into 4 equal squares.
3. Spread about 2 tablespoons of tomato sauce onto one half of each puff pastry square, leaving a small border around the edges.
4. Sprinkle grated mozzarella cheese over the tomato sauce on each square.
5. Place a few slices of pepperoni or cooked ham and

some sliced black olives on top of the cheese.
6. Sprinkle dried oregano, garlic powder, and onion powder evenly over the toppings.
7. Fold the other half of each puff pastry square over the toppings to form a pocket. Use a fork to press the edges together and seal the pockets.
8. Lightly brush the tops of the pizza pockets with olive oil.
9. Place the pizza pockets in the air fryer basket, leaving space between them for even cooking.
10. Air fry the pizza pockets at 180°C for 8-10 minutes, or until the pastry is golden brown and crispy.
11. Once cooked, remove the pizza pockets from the air fryer and let them cool for a few minutes before serving.
12. Garnish with fresh basil leaves, if desired, and serve the mini pizza pockets as a delicious and convenient meal.

Air Fryer Grilled Cheese Sandwich

Prep Time: 5 minutes / Cook Time: 5-6 minutes
Serves: 4

Ingredients:

- 4 slices of bread of your choice
- 100 g of cheddar cheese, shredded
- 100 g of mozzarella cheese, shredded
- 2 tablespoons of unsalted butter, melted
- Salt and pepper to taste

Instructions:

1. Preheat the Air Fryer to 180°C.
2. In a bowl, mix together the cheddar and mozzarella cheese.
3. Take two slices of bread and spread melted butter on one side of each slice.
4. Sprinkle a pinch of salt and pepper on the buttered side of each slice of bread.
5. Place a generous amount of cheese mixture on top of one slice of bread, then place the other slice of bread on top, buttered side facing out. Repeat the same steps for the remaining slices of bread.
6. Place the sandwiches in the Air Fryer basket. Make sure they are not touching each other.
7. Cook the sandwiches for 5-6 minutes or until they are golden brown and the cheese is melted.
8. Once done, remove from the Air Fryer and let it cool for a minute.
9. Cut the sandwich in halves or quarters and serve with your favourite dipping sauce. Enjoy!

Chapter 8 Appetisers

Cheese and Onion Tartlets

Prep Time: 20 minutes / Cook Time: 25 minutes
Serves: 4

Ingredients:

- 320g puff pastry
- 1 large onion, thinly sliced
- 1 tablespoon butter
- 150g grated cheese (e.g., Cheddar, Gruyere, or a mix)
- 2 eggs
- 150ml heavy cream
- Salt and pepper, to taste
- Fresh thyme leaves, for garnish (optional)

Instructions:

1. Preheat the air fryer oven to 200°C. Grease four individual tartlet pans or a tart tin.
2. Roll out the puff pastry on a floured surface to a thickness of about 3-4 mm.
3. Cut out circles of pastry slightly larger than the tartlet pans or tin. Press the pastry circles into the pans, trimming any excess.
4. In a skillet, melt the butter over medium heat. Add the thinly sliced onion and cook for about 5-7 minutes until softened and lightly caramelised. Remove from heat and let it cool slightly.
5. In a bowl, whisk together the eggs and heavy cream. Season with salt and pepper.
6. Sprinkle the grated cheese evenly over the bottom of the pastry shells.
7. Distribute the caramelised onions over the cheese.
8. Pour the egg and cream mixture over the onions and cheese, filling each tartlet shell almost to the top.
9. Place the tartlet pans or tin on a baking sheet and transfer to the preheated air fryer oven.
10. Bake for approximately 20-25 minutes or until the tartlets are golden brown and set in the centre.
11. Remove from the air fryer oven and let them cool slightly.
12. Garnish with fresh thyme leaves, if desired.
13. Serve the cheese and onion tartlets warm or at room temperature as an appetiser or light lunch.

Bruschetta with Tomato and Basil

Prep Time: 15 minutes / Cook Time: 5 minutes
Serves: 4

Ingredients:

- 4 slices of baguette or Italian bread
- 2 large tomatoes, diced
- 2 cloves of garlic, minced
- 8 fresh basil leaves, torn
- 2 tablespoons extra virgin olive oil
- Salt and pepper, to taste
- Balsamic glaze, for drizzling (optional)

Instructions:

1. Preheat the air fryer medium-high heat.
2. Place the slices of bread on a baking sheet and toast them under the air fryer broiler for about 2-3 minutes on each side until lightly golden and crisp.
3. In a bowl, combine the diced tomatoes, minced garlic, torn basil leaves, and extra virgin olive oil. Season with salt and pepper to taste. Toss well to combine.
4. Remove the toasted bread from the air fryer oven and let it cool slightly.
5. Rub each slice of bread with a clove of garlic to impart a subtle garlic flavour.
6. Spoon the tomato and basil mixture onto each bread slice, spreading it evenly.
7. Drizzle with balsamic glaze, if desired, for added sweetness and tanginess.
8. Serve the bruschetta with tomato and basil immediately as an appetiser or light snack.

Bacon-Wrapped Dates with Goat Cheese

Prep Time: 15 minutes / Cook Time: 15 minutes
Serves: 4

Ingredients:

- 12 Medjool dates
- 12 slices of bacon, cut in half lengthwise
- 100g goat cheese
- Fresh basil leaves, for garnish (optional)

Instructions:

1. Preheat the air fryer oven to 200°C. Line a baking sheet with parchment paper.
2. Make a small incision on one side of each date and remove the pit.
3. Stuff each date with a small amount of goat cheese, using a teaspoon or your fingers.
4. Wrap each stuffed date with a halved slice of bacon, securing it with a toothpick if needed.
5. Place the bacon-wrapped dates on the prepared baking sheet, seam-side down.
6. Bake in the preheated air fryer oven for about 12-15 minutes, or until the bacon is crispy and golden.
7. Remove from the air fryer oven and let them cool slightly.

8. Garnish with fresh basil leaves, if desired, for added freshness and aroma.
9. Serve the bacon-wrapped dates with goat cheese warm as an appetiser or part of a charcuterie board.

Mini Vegetable Samosas with Mango Chutney

Prep Time: 30 minutes / Cook Time: 20 minutes
Serves: 4

Ingredients:

For the samosas:
- 12 small samosa pastry sheets
- 150g mixed vegetables (such as peas, carrots, potatoes, and corn), boiled and mashed
- 1 small onion, finely chopped
- 2 cloves of garlic, minced
- 1 teaspoon ginger, grated
- 1 teaspoon cumin seeds
- 1 teaspoon coriander powder
- 1/2 teaspoon turmeric powder
- 1/2 teaspoon garam masala
- Salt, to taste
- Vegetable oil, for frying

For the mango chutney:
- 1 ripe mango, peeled and diced
- 1 tablespoon lemon juice
- 1 tablespoon brown sugar
- 1/2 teaspoon chilli flakes (optional)

Instructions:

1. In a pan, heat a tablespoon of vegetable oil over medium heat.
2. Add the cumin seeds and Sauté for a minute until they start to sizzle.
3. Add the chopped onion, minced garlic, and grated ginger. Cook until the onion turns translucent.
4. Add the mashed vegetables, coriander powder, turmeric powder, garam masala, and salt. Mix well to combine.
5. Cook the vegetable mixture for about 3-4 minutes, stirring occasionally, until the flavours meld together. Remove from heat and let it cool.
6. Take a samosa pastry sheet and fold it into a cone shape, leaving a small opening at the top.
7. Fill the cone with a tablespoon of the vegetable filling. Moisten the edges of the pastry with water and seal the top, pressing gently to ensure it sticks.
8. Repeat the process with the remaining samosa pastry sheets and vegetable filling.
9. Heat vegetable oil in a deep fryer or a deep saucepan over medium-high heat. If using an air fryer, preheat it according to the manufacturer's instructions.
10. Preheat the air fryer according to the manufacturer's instructions and place the samosas in a single layer in the air fryer basket. Cook at 180° for about 10-12 minutes, flipping halfway through, until they are crispy and cooked through.
11. Remove the fried or air-fried samosas from the oil or air fryer and drain them on a paper towel to remove excess oil.
12. For the mango chutney, in a small bowl, combine the diced mango, lemon juice, brown sugar, and chilli flakes (if using). Mix well to coat the mango with the flavours.
13. Serve the mini vegetable samosas hot with mango chutney on the side for dipping.

Mini Crab Cakes with Lemon Aioli

Prep Time: 20 minutes / Cook Time: 15 minutes
Serves: 4

Ingredients:

For the crab cakes:
- 200g crab meat
- 60g breadcrumbs
- 2 tablespoons mayonnaise
- 1 tablespoon Dijon mustard
- 1 tablespoon fresh parsley, finely chopped
- 1 tablespoon fresh chives, finely chopped
- 1/2 teaspoon Old Bay seasoning (or substitute with paprika and a pinch of cayenne pepper)
- Salt and pepper, to taste
- 1 egg, beaten
- 2 tablespoons vegetable oil, for frying

For the lemon aioli:
- 120ml mayonnaise
- 1 tablespoon lemon juice
- 1/2 teaspoon lemon zest
- 1 clove garlic, minced
- Salt and pepper, to taste

Instructions:

1. In a mixing bowl, combine the crab meat, breadcrumbs, mayonnaise, Dijon mustard, parsley, chives, Old Bay seasoning, salt, and pepper. Mix well to combine.
2. Form the mixture into small patties, about 2-3 inches in diameter.
3. Heat vegetable oil in a frying pan over medium heat.
4. Dip each crab cake patty into the beaten egg, coating it evenly, and then place it in the hot pan.
5. Cook the crab cakes for about 3-4 minutes on each side, or until golden brown and crispy. Be careful not to overcrowd the pan; cook in batches if necessary.
6. Remove the cooked crab cakes from the pan and drain on a paper towel to remove excess oil.
7. In a small bowl, whisk together the mayonnaise, lemon juice, lemon zest, minced garlic, salt, and pepper to make the lemon aioli.
8. Serve the mini crab cakes hot with a dollop of lemon aioli on top. Garnish with additional chopped parsley or chives, if desired.

Potted Shrimp on Toasted Sourdough

Prep Time: 15 minutes / Cook Time: 10 minutes
Serves: 4

Ingredients:

- 250g cooked peeled shrimp
- 100g unsalted butter
- 1 shallot, finely chopped
- 1 clove garlic, minced
- 1/2 teaspoon ground nutmeg
- 1/2 teaspoon ground mace
- 1/2 teaspoon paprika
- Zest of 1 lemon
- Salt and pepper, to taste
- Sourdough bread slices, toasted, for serving

Instructions:

1. In a saucepan, melt the butter over medium heat.
2. Add the chopped shallot and minced garlic to the pan. Sauté for a few minutes until the shallot becomes translucent.
3. Stir in the ground nutmeg, ground mace, paprika, lemon zest, salt, and pepper. Cook for another minute to let the flavours meld together.
4. Add the cooked peeled shrimp to the pan and stir well to coat them with the seasoned butter. Cook for 2-3 minutes until the shrimp are heated through.
5. Remove the pan from heat and let the mixture cool slightly.
6. Spoon the shrimp mixture into small ramekins or jars, packing it down lightly.
7. Place the ramekins or jars in the refrigerator to chill for at least 1 hour, allowing it to cool.
8. Once chilled, remove the potted shrimp from the refrigerator and serve on toasted sourdough bread slices.
9. Garnish with a sprinkle of fresh parsley or chives, if desired.

Mini Spinach and Feta Puffs

Prep Time: 20 minutes / Cook Time: 20 minutes
Serves: 4

Ingredients:

- 1 sheet puff pastry, thawed
- 150g fresh spinach leaves, roughly chopped
- 100g feta cheese, crumbled
- 25g grated Parmesan cheese
- 1 small onion, finely chopped
- 2 cloves garlic, minced
- 1 tablespoon olive oil
- 1/2 teaspoon dried oregano
- Salt and pepper, to taste
- 1 egg, beaten (for egg wash)

Instructions:

1. Preheat the air fryer oven to 200°C and line a baking sheet with parchment paper.
2. Heat olive oil in a skillet over medium heat. Add the chopped onion and minced garlic, and Sauté until the onion becomes translucent, about 3-4 minutes.
3. Add the chopped spinach to the skillet and cook until wilted, stirring occasionally. Remove from heat and let cool slightly.
4. In a mixing bowl, combine the cooked spinach and onion mixture with crumbled feta cheese, grated Parmesan cheese, dried oregano, salt, and pepper. Mix well to incorporate all the ingredients.
5. Roll out the puff pastry sheet onto a lightly floured surface. Cut the pastry into small squares or circles, about 3 inches in size.
6. Place a spoonful of the spinach and feta mixture onto the centre of each pastry square. Fold the pastry over the filling to form a triangle or turnover shape. Use a fork to seal the edges.
7. Arrange the filled pastry puffs on the prepared baking sheet. Brush the tops with beaten egg for a golden finish.
8. Bake in the preheated air fryer oven for 15-20 minutes, or until the pastry turns golden brown and puffs up.
9. Remove from the air fryer oven and let the mini spinach and feta puffs cool for a few minutes before serving.

Crispy Fried Oysters with Tartar Sauce

Prep Time: 30 minutes / Cook Time: 10 minutes
Serves: 4

Ingredients:

- For the crispy fried oysters:
- 24 fresh oysters, shucked
- 100g all-purpose flour
- 2 eggs, beaten
- 100g breadcrumbs
- 1/2 teaspoon paprika
- Salt and pepper, to taste
- Vegetable oil, for deep frying
- For the tartar sauce:
- 150g mayonnaise
- 2 tablespoons finely chopped pickles
- 1 tablespoon capers, drained and chopped
- 1 tablespoon lemon juice
- 1 teaspoon Dijon mustard
- 1 tablespoon finely chopped fresh dill
- Salt and pepper, to taste

Instructions:

1. In a bowl, combine the all-purpose flour with a pinch of salt and pepper. In another bowl, place the beaten eggs. In a third bowl, mix the breadcrumbs with

paprika, salt, and pepper.

2. Dip each shucked oyster into the flour, shaking off any excess. Then dip it into the beaten eggs, allowing any excess to drip off. Finally, coat the oyster in the seasoned breadcrumbs, pressing gently to adhere. Repeat this process for all the oysters.

3. Heat vegetable oil in a deep fryer or large heavy-bottomed pot to 180°C. Carefully add a few coated oysters at a time into the hot oil and fry until golden brown and crispy, about 2-3 minutes. Use a slotted spoon to transfer the fried oysters to a plate lined with paper towels to drain excess oil. Repeat until all the oysters are fried.

4. In a small bowl, prepare the tartar sauce by combining mayonnaise, chopped pickles, capers, lemon juice, Dijon mustard, chopped dill, salt, and pepper. Mix well to combine.

5. Serve the crispy fried oysters hot with a side of tartar sauce for dipping.

Stuffed Baby Potatoes with Sour Cream and Chives

Prep Time: 20 minutes / Cook Time: 30 minutes
Serves: 4

Ingredients:

- 16 baby potatoes (around 500g)
- 2 tablespoons olive oil
- Salt and pepper, to taste
- 150g sour cream
- 2 tablespoons fresh chives, finely chopped
- Optional toppings: grated cheese, crispy bacon bits, sliced green onions

Instructions:

1. Preheat the air fryer oven to 200°C and line a baking sheet with parchment paper.

2. Rinse the baby potatoes and pat them dry. Place them on the prepared baking sheet.

3. Drizzle the potatoes with olive oil and season with salt and pepper. Toss them gently to coat evenly.

4. Roast the potatoes in the preheated air fryer oven for about 25-30 minutes, or until they are tender and golden brown. Turn them once halfway through the cooking time for even browning.

5. Remove the potatoes from the air fryer oven and let them cool slightly.

6. Cut a small slice off the top of each potato to create a flat surface. Using a small spoon or melon baller, scoop out a small amount of flesh from each potato, creating a cavity for the filling. Reserve the scooped-out potato flesh for another use or discard.

7. In a bowl, mix the sour cream and chopped chives. Season with salt and pepper to taste.

8. Fill each potato cavity with the sour cream and chive

mixture, using a spoon or piping bag.

9. If desired, top the stuffed potatoes with grated cheese, crispy bacon bits, or sliced green onions for extra flavour and presentation.

10. Place the stuffed potatoes back in the air fryer oven for another 5 minutes, or until the filling is heated through and the toppings are melted and crispy.

11. Serve the stuffed baby potatoes as a delightful appetiser or side dish. They can be enjoyed warm or at room temperature.

Wontons with Sweet chilli Sauce

Prep Time: 30 minutes / Cook Time: 10 minutes
Serves: 4-6

Ingredients:

- For the Wontons:
- 250g ground pork
- 150g shrimp, peeled and deveined, finely chopped
- 2 spring onions, finely chopped
- 1 clove of garlic, minced
- 1 teaspoon ginger, grated
- 1 tablespoon soy sauce
- 1 tablespoon oyster sauce
- 1 teaspoon sesame oil
- 30-40 wonton wrappers
- Water for sealing
- For the Sweet Chilli Sauce:
- 3 tablespoons sweet chilli sauce
- 1 tablespoon soy sauce
- 1 tablespoon rice vinegar
- 1 teaspoon honey
- 1/2 teaspoon sesame oil
- 1 spring onion, finely chopped (for garnish)

Instructions:

1. In a mixing bowl, combine the ground pork, chopped shrimp, spring onions, minced garlic, grated ginger, soy sauce, oyster sauce, and sesame oil. Mix well until all the ingredients are thoroughly combined.

2. Place a small spoonful of the pork and shrimp mixture in the centre of a wonton wrapper.

3. Moisten the edges of the wrapper with water using your finger or a brush.

4. Fold the wonton wrapper in half diagonally to form a triangle, pressing the edges together to seal tightly.

5. Bring the two corners of the triangle together and overlap them slightly, sealing them with a little water to form the classic wonton shape. Repeat this process for the remaining wrappers and filling.

6. In a large pot, bring water to a boil. Add a pinch of salt to the water.

7. Carefully drop the wontons into the boiling water, ensuring they don't stick together. Cook for about 3-4 minutes, or until the wontons float to the surface and

are cooked through.

8. Using a slotted spoon, remove the cooked wontons from the pot and transfer them to a serving platter or individual bowls.
9. In a small bowl, whisk together the sweet chilli sauce, soy sauce, rice vinegar, honey, and sesame oil to make the sweet chilli sauce.
10. Drizzle the sweet chilli sauce over the cooked wontons.
11. Garnish with finely chopped spring onions.
12. Serve the wontons with sweet chilli sauce hot as an appetiser or part of a meal.

Mini Baked Brie with Red Onion

Prep Time: 10 minutes / Cook Time: 20 minutes
Serves: 4-6

Ingredients:

- 1 small wheel of Brie cheese
- 1 red onion, thinly sliced
- 2 tablespoons balsamic vinegar
- 1 tablespoon olive oil
- 1 tablespoon brown sugar
- Fresh thyme sprigs, for garnish (optional)
- Crackers or sliced baguette, for serving

Instructions:

1. Preheat your air fryer to 180°C.
2. Slice the top rind of the Brie cheese wheel to expose the cheese inside. Place the Brie wheel in a baking dish or on a baking sheet lined with parchment paper.
3. In a small bowl, mix the sliced red onion, balsamic vinegar, olive oil, and brown sugar together until well combined.
4. Spread the onion mixture evenly over the top of the Brie wheel.
5. Bake the Brie in the preheated air fryer oven for about 15-20 minutes, or until the cheese is melted and bubbly.
6. Carefully remove the baked Brie from the air fryer oven and let it cool for a few minutes.
7. Garnish with fresh thyme sprigs, if desired, for added aroma and visual appeal.
8. Serve the mini baked Brie with red onion hot, accompanied by crackers or sliced baguette for spreading the warm, gooey cheese.

Bruschetta with Pea and Mint Pesto

Prep Time: 15 minutes / Cook Time: 10 minutes
Serves: 4-6

Ingredients:

- 1 French baguette, sliced diagonally into 2.5 cm thick pieces
- 200g fresh or frozen peas
- 30g fresh mint leaves
- 30g grated Parmesan cheese
- 30g pine nuts
- 2 cloves of garlic, minced
- 60ml extra virgin olive oil
- Salt and pepper, to taste

Instructions:

1. Preheat the air fryer to medium-high heat.
2. In a pot of boiling water, cook the peas for about 2-3 minutes until they are tender. If using frozen peas, follow the package instructions.
3. Drain the cooked peas and transfer them to a food processor or blender.
4. Add the fresh mint leaves, grated Parmesan cheese, pine nuts, minced garlic, and extra virgin olive oil to the peas.
5. Pulse the mixture until you reach a smooth and creamy consistency. You may need to scrape down the sides of the processor or blender a few times to ensure everything is well combined.
6. Season the pea and mint pesto with salt and pepper to taste. Adjust the seasoning according to your preference.
7. Place the baguette slices on a baking sheet and drizzle them with a little olive oil.
8. Toast the baguette slices under the preheated air fryer broiler for about 2-3 minutes on each side, or until they are golden brown and crispy.
9. Remove the toasted baguette slices from the air fryer oven and let them cool slightly.
10. Spread a generous amount of the pea and mint pesto onto each toasted baguette slice.
11. Serve the bruschetta with pea and mint pesto as an appetiser or light snack.

Smoked Trout and Horseradish

Prep Time: 10 minutes / Cook Time: 5 minutes
Serves: 4-6

Ingredients:

- 1 French baguette, sliced diagonally into 1-inch thick pieces
- 200g smoked trout fillets
- 4 tablespoons prepared horseradish
- 2 tablespoons sour cream
- 1 tablespoon lemon juice
- 1 tablespoon fresh dill, chopped
- Salt and pepper, to taste

Instructions:

1. Preheat the air fryer to medium-high heat.
2. In a small bowl, combine the prepared horseradish, sour cream, lemon juice, and chopped fresh dill. Mix well to create the horseradish sauce. Season with salt and pepper to taste.
3. Place the baguette slices on a baking sheet and drizzle

them with a little olive oil.

4. Toast the baguette slices under the preheated air fryer broiler for about 2-3 minutes on each side, or until they are golden brown and crispy.

5. Remove the toasted baguette slices from the air fryer oven and let them cool slightly.

6. Flake the smoked trout fillets into bite-sized pieces, removing any skin or bones.

7. Spread a thin layer of the horseradish sauce onto each toasted baguette slice.

8. Top the horseradish sauce with the flaked smoked trout pieces.

9. Garnish with additional fresh dill, if desired.

10. Serve the smoked trout and horseradish bruschetta as an appetiser or light snack.

Mozzarella and Tomato Arancini Balls

Prep Time: 30 minutes / Cook Time: 20 minutes
Serves: 4-6

Ingredients:

- 300g Arborio rice
- 1 onion, finely chopped
- 2 cloves of garlic, minced
- 800ml vegetable broth or stock
- 100g mozzarella cheese, cut into small cubes
- 2 ripe tomatoes, seeded and diced
- 50g grated Parmesan cheese
- 2 tablespoons fresh basil leaves, chopped
- 2 eggs, beaten
- 150g breadcrumbs
- Vegetable oil, for frying
- Salt and pepper, to taste

Instructions:

1. In a large saucepan, heat a little vegetable oil over medium heat. Add the chopped onion and minced garlic, and Sauté until the onion becomes translucent and the garlic is fragrant.

2. Add the Arborio rice to the pan and stir it around for a minute to coat it with the oil and onion mixture.

3. Gradually pour in the vegetable broth or stock, about 200ml at a time, stirring constantly. Allow each addition of broth to be absorbed before adding more. Continue this process until the rice is cooked and creamy, which should take about 20 minutes.

4. Remove the risotto from the heat and let it cool slightly. Then, transfer it to a large mixing bowl.

5. Add the mozzarella cheese cubes, diced tomatoes, grated Parmesan cheese, and chopped basil to the risotto. Season with salt and pepper to taste. Mix well until all the ingredients are evenly distributed.

6. Take a handful of the risotto mixture and shape it into a ball, about the size of a golf ball. Make an indentation in the centre of the ball and place a small piece of mozzarella cheese inside. Close the rice around the cheese, ensuring it is completely sealed. Repeat this process until all the mixture is used.

7. Dip each arancini ball into the beaten eggs, then roll it in the breadcrumbs, making sure it is evenly coated. Place the coated balls on a baking sheet lined with parchment paper.

8. Heat vegetable oil in the air fryer or large pot to 180°C. Carefully lower a few arancini balls into the hot oil and fry them until golden brown and crispy, usually about 4-5 minutes. Remove them with a slotted spoon and place them on a paper towel-lined plate to drain excess oil. Repeat this process with the remaining arancini balls.

9. Serve the mozzarella and tomato arancini balls hot as an appetiser or a delicious snack. They can be enjoyed on their own or with a dipping sauce of your choice.

Goat Cheese and Beetroot Crostini

Prep Time: 15 minutes / Cook Time: 15 minutes
Serves: 4-6

Ingredients:

- 1 French baguette, sliced diagonally into 1-inch thick pieces
- 200g goat cheese
- 2 medium-sized beetroots, cooked and peeled
- 2 tablespoons honey
- 1 tablespoon balsamic vinegar
- Fresh thyme leaves, for garnish (optional)

Instructions:

1. Preheat your air fryer to 180°C.

2. Place the baguette slices on a baking sheet and drizzle them with a little olive oil. Bake in the preheated air fryer oven for about 10-12 minutes, or until they are crispy and lightly golden brown. Remove from the air fryer oven and let them cool slightly.

3. In a small bowl, mash the goat cheese with a fork until it becomes smooth and spreadable.

4. Cut the cooked beetroots into thin slices.

5. Spread a layer of the mashed goat cheese onto each toasted baguette slice.

6. Top the goat cheese with a slice of beetroot.

7. Drizzle a little honey and balsamic vinegar over each crostini.

8. Garnish with fresh thyme leaves, if desired, for added aroma and visual appeal.

9. Serve the goat cheese and beetroot crostini as an elegant appetiser or a light snack.

Mini Teriyaki Chicken Skewers

Prep Time: 15 minutes / Marinating Time: 1 hour /
Cook Time: 10 minutes
Serves: 4-6

Ingredients:

- 500g boneless, skinless chicken breasts, cut into small bite-sized pieces
- 4 tablespoons soy sauce
- 2 tablespoons honey
- 2 tablespoons mirin (Japanese sweet rice wine)
- 2 tablespoons rice vinegar
- 1 tablespoon sesame oil
- 1 tablespoon grated fresh ginger
- 2 cloves of garlic, minced
- Wooden skewers, soaked in water for 30 minutes

Instructions:

1. In a mixing bowl, combine the soy sauce, honey, mirin, rice vinegar, sesame oil, grated ginger, and minced garlic. Stir well to combine and create the teriyaki marinade.
2. Add the chicken pieces to the marinade, ensuring they are well coated. Cover the bowl with plastic wrap and let it marinate in the refrigerator for at least 1 hour, or overnight for enhanced flavour.
3. Preheat the air fryer to medium-high heat.
4. Thread the marinated chicken pieces onto the soaked wooden skewers, leaving a little space between each piece.
5. Place the chicken skewers on the preheated air fryer. Cook for about 4-5 minutes on each side, or until the chicken is cooked through and slightly charred. Baste the skewers with the remaining marinade while cooking.
6. Once cooked, remove the chicken skewers from the air fryer broiler and let them rest for a few minutes.
7. Serve the mini teriyaki chicken skewers as an appetiser or part of a main course. They pair well with steamed rice or a side salad.

Baked Brie with Fig Jam and Almonds

Prep Time: 10 minutes / Cook Time: 15 minutes
Serves: 4-6

Ingredients:

- 1 round of Brie cheese (about 250g)
- 4 tablespoons fig jam
- 2 tablespoons sliced almonds
- Crackers or sliced baguette, for serving

Instructions:

1. Preheat your air fryer to 180°C.
2. Place the round of Brie cheese on a baking sheet lined with parchment paper.
3. Spread the fig jam evenly over the top of the Brie cheese.
4. Sprinkle the sliced almonds over the fig jam, covering the surface.
5. Bake in the preheated air fryer oven for about 12-15 minutes, or until the Brie cheese is soft and gooey, and the almonds are lightly toasted.

6. Remove from the air fryer oven and let it cool for a few minutes before serving.
7. Serve the baked Brie with fig jam and almonds as an appetiser or part of a cheese platter. Accompany it with crackers or sliced baguette for spreading and dipping.

Vegetable Tempura with Soy Dipping Sauce

Prep Time: 15 minutes / Cook Time: 15 minutes
Serves: 4-6

Ingredients:

For Vegetable Tempura:
- Assorted vegetables (such as zucchini, bell peppers, sweet potatoes, broccoli florets, and mushrooms), sliced into bite-sized pieces
- 150g all-purpose flour
- 2 tablespoons cornstarch
- 1/2 teaspoon baking powder
- 1/2 teaspoon salt
- 240ml ice-cold water
- Vegetable oil, for deep frying

For Soy Dipping Sauce:
- 4 tablespoons soy sauce
- 2 tablespoons rice vinegar
- 2 teaspoons honey or maple syrup
- 1 teaspoon grated ginger
- 1 teaspoon sesame oil
- 1 tablespoon chopped green onions (optional)
- Toasted sesame seeds, for garnish (optional)

Instructions:

1. In a mixing bowl, whisk together the all-purpose flour, cornstarch, baking powder, and salt.
2. Gradually add the ice-cold water to the flour mixture, whisking until you have a smooth batter. The batter should be thin enough to coat the vegetables but not too runny.
3. Heat vegetable oil in a deep fryer or large pot to 180°C.
4. Dip the vegetable pieces into the batter, coating them evenly. Allow any excess batter to drip off before carefully placing them into the hot oil. Fry a few pieces at a time, ensuring they do not stick together.
5. Fry the vegetables for about 2-3 minutes, or until they turn golden brown and crispy. Use a slotted spoon or tongs to remove them from the oil and transfer to a paper towel-lined plate to drain excess oil.
6. Repeat the frying process with the remaining vegetable pieces until they are all cooked.
7. For the soy dipping sauce, whisk together the soy sauce, rice vinegar, honey or maple syrup, grated ginger, sesame oil, and chopped green onions in a small bowl. Adjust the sweetness or acidity according to your taste preference.
8. Serve the vegetable tempura hot with the soy dipping sauce on the side. Sprinkle with toasted sesame seeds for added flavour and presentation, if desired.

Chapter 9 Snacks and Desserts

Apricot Tart

Prep Time: 20 minutes / Cook Time: 40 minutes
Serves: 8

Ingredients:

For the Tart Crust:
- 200g all-purpose flour
- 100g unsalted butter, cold and cubed
- 50g granulated sugar
- 1 large egg, lightly beaten
- 1/2 teaspoon vanilla extract
- Pinch of salt

For the Apricot Filling:
- 500g fresh apricots, halved and pitted
- 50g granulated sugar
- 1 tablespoon lemon juice
- 1 teaspoon lemon zest

For the Glaze:
- 2 tablespoons apricot jam
- 1 tablespoon water

Instructions:

1. Preheat your air fryer to 180°C.
2. In a large bowl, combine the flour, butter, sugar, egg, vanilla extract, and salt. Use your fingertips or a pastry cutter to rub the butter into the flour until the mixture resembles coarse crumbs.
3. Gather the dough into a ball and lightly knead it until it comes together. Wrap the dough in plastic wrap and refrigerate for 30 minutes.
4. On a lightly floured surface, roll out the chilled dough to fit a 9-inch tart pan. Press the dough into the pan, making sure to evenly distribute it along the bottom and sides. Trim any excess dough.
5. Arrange the apricot halves, cut side up, in the prepared tart crust.
6. In a small bowl, mix together the granulated sugar, lemon juice, and lemon zest. Drizzle this mixture evenly over the apricots.
7. Bake the tart in the preheated air fryer oven for 40 minutes, or until the crust is golden brown and the apricots are tender.
8. In a small saucepan, heat the apricot jam and water over low heat until melted and smooth. Remove from heat.
9. Once the tart is done, remove it from the air fryer oven and brush the top of the apricots with the apricot glaze.
10. Allow the tart to cool slightly before serving. It can be served warm or at room temperature.

Treacle Tart

Prep Time: 20 minutes / Cook Time: 40 minutes
Serves: 8-10

Ingredients:

For the pastry:
- 250g all-purpose flour
- 125g unsalted butter, cold and cubed
- 50g icing sugar
- 1 large egg, beaten
- 2-3 tablespoons cold water

For the filling:
- 450g golden syrup
- 150g fresh white breadcrumbs
- Zest and juice of 1 lemon
- 1 teaspoon ground ginger (optional)

Instructions:

1. Preheat your air fryer to 180°C.
2. In a large mixing bowl, combine the flour and icing sugar. Add the cold cubed butter and rub it into the flour mixture until it resembles breadcrumbs.
3. Make a well in the centre of the mixture and pour in the beaten egg. Gradually mix in the egg using a fork or your fingers, then add enough cold water, a tablespoon at a time, to bring the mixture together into a firm dough.
4. Turn the dough out onto a lightly floured surface and knead it gently until smooth. Wrap it in cling film and refrigerate for 30 minutes.
5. Meanwhile, in a saucepan, heat the golden syrup over low heat until it becomes runny. Remove from the heat and stir in the fresh white breadcrumbs, lemon zest, lemon juice, and ground ginger (if using). Mix well to combine.
6. On a lightly floured surface, roll out the chilled pastry to fit a 9-inch tart tin. Carefully line the tin with the pastry, pressing it into the edges and trimming any excess.
7. Pour the treacle filling into the pastry case, spreading it out evenly.
8. Place the tart on a baking sheet and bake in the preheated air fryer oven for about 40 minutes, or until the pastry is golden brown and the filling is set.
9. Remove from the air fryer oven and allow the treacle tart to cool slightly before serving.
10. Serve the treacle tart warm or at room temperature. It pairs well with a dollop of clotted cream or a scoop of vanilla ice cream.

Chocolate Fondant

Prep Time: 20 minutes / Cook time: 12 minutes
Serves: 4

Ingredients:

- 150g dark chocolate (at least 70% cocoa solids)
- 150g unsalted butter, plus extra for greasing
- 150g powdered sugar
- 3 large eggs
- 3 large egg yolks
- 75g all-purpose flour
- Cocoa powder, for dusting
- Vanilla ice cream or whipped cream, for serving (optional)
- Fresh berries, for garnish (optional)
- Mint leaves, for garnish (optional)

Instructions:

1. Preheat your oven to 200°C. Grease four ramekins or small oven-safe dishes with butter, then dust them with cocoa powder, tapping out any excess.
2. Break the dark chocolate into small pieces and place them in a heatproof bowl. Add the butter to the bowl. Set the bowl over a pot of simmering water, making sure the bottom of the bowl doesn't touch the water. Stir the chocolate and butter until melted and smooth. Remove from heat and set aside to cool slightly.
3. In a separate mixing bowl, whisk together the powdered sugar, eggs, and egg yolks until well combined.
4. Gradually pour the chocolate mixture into the egg mixture, whisking constantly until smooth and fully incorporated.
5. Sift the flour into the bowl and gently fold it into the chocolate mixture until just combined. Be careful not to overmix.
6. Divide the batter equally among the prepared ramekins, filling them about three-fourths full.
7. Place the ramekins on a baking sheet and bake in the preheated oven for 10-12 minutes. The edges should be set, but the centre should still be slightly wobbly.
8. Remove the fondants from the oven and let them cool in the ramekins for a minute or two. Then, using a butter knife, carefully loosen the edges and invert each fondant onto a serving plate.
9. Serve the chocolate fondants immediately while they are still warm. You can garnish them with a dusting of powdered sugar, a scoop of vanilla ice cream or whipped cream, fresh berries, or mint leaves.
10. Break into the fondants with a spoon to release the gooey chocolate centre and enjoy!

Chocolate Eclairs

Prep Time: 30 minutes / Cook Time: 30 minutes
Serves: 10-12

Ingredients:

For the Choux Pastry:
- 120ml water
- 60g unsalted butter
- 70g all-purpose flour
- 2 large eggs

For the Cream Filling:
- 500ml whole milk
- 4 large egg yolks
- 100g granulated sugar
- 40g cornstarch
- 1 teaspoon vanilla extract
- 250ml whipping cream

For the Chocolate Glaze:
- 150g dark chocolate, chopped
- 120ml whipping cream
- 1 tablespoon unsalted butter

Instructions:

1. Preheat your air fryer to 200°C. Line a baking sheet with parchment paper.
2. In a saucepan, bring the water and butter to a boil over medium heat. Once the butter has melted, remove the pan from heat and quickly stir in the flour until well combined.
3. Return the saucepan to low heat and cook the mixture for 1-2 minutes, stirring constantly, until it forms a smooth ball of dough and pulls away from the sides of the pan.
4. Transfer the dough to a mixing bowl and let it cool for a few minutes. Then, using an electric mixer or a wooden spoon, beat in the eggs one at a time until the dough becomes smooth and glossy.
5. Transfer the choux pastry dough into a piping bag fitted with a large round tip.
6. Pipe 3-4 inch long strips of dough onto the prepared baking sheet, leaving enough space between each eclair for them to expand.
7. Bake in the preheated air fryer oven for 20-25 minutes, or until the eclairs are puffed up and golden brown. Then, reduce the air fryer oven temperature to 180° and continue baking for an additional 5-10 minutes to dry out the centres.
8. Remove the eclairs from the air fryer oven and let them cool completely on a wire rack.
9. Meanwhile, prepare the cream filling. In a saucepan, heat the milk over medium heat until hot but not boiling.
10. In a separate bowl, whisk together the egg yolks, sugar, cornstarch, and vanilla extract until smooth and well combined.

11. Gradually pour the hot milk into the egg mixture while whisking constantly to temper the eggs. Then, pour the mixture back into the saucepan and cook over medium heat, stirring constantly, until it thickens and comes to a boil.
12. Remove the saucepan from heat and transfer the cream filling to a bowl. Cover the surface with plastic wrap to prevent a skin from forming. Let it cool completely.
13. In a separate bowl, whip the whipping cream until stiff peaks form. Gently fold the whipped cream into the cooled cream filling until well combined.
14. Using a piping bag fitted with a small round tip, fill each eclair with the cream filling by making a small hole on one side and piping the cream inside.
15. For the chocolate glaze, place the chopped dark chocolate in a heatproof bowl. In a saucepan, heat the whipping cream until it begins to simmer. Pour the hot cream over the chocolate and let it sit for a minute. Then, add the butter and stir until the mixture is smooth and glossy.
16. Dip the top of each filled eclair into the chocolate glaze, allowing any excess to drip off. Place the eclairs on a wire rack to set.
17. Refrigerate the chocolate eclairs for at least 1 hour before serving to allow the filling to set and the flavours to meld together.
18. Serve the chocolate eclairs and enjoy! These delightful pastries are best enjoyed fresh. The crisp choux pastry filled with creamy vanilla filling and topped with luscious chocolate glaze will surely satisfy your sweet tooth.
19. Optional: For added decoration, you can drizzle some extra chocolate glaze over the top of the eclairs or sprinkle them with powdered sugar.
20. Store any leftover chocolate eclairs in the refrigerator, covered, for up to 2-3 days. However, note that the pastry may soften slightly over time.

Pistachio Rosewater Cupcakes

Prep Time: 20 minutes / Cook time: 20 minutes
Serves: 12 cupcakes

Ingredients:

For the cupcakes:
- 150g unsalted butter, softened
- 150g granulated sugar
- 3 large eggs
- 150g all-purpose flour
- 1 teaspoon baking powder
- 1/4 teaspoon salt
- 75g ground pistachios
- 1 teaspoon rosewater
- 120mls milk

For the frosting:
- 250 grams powdered sugar
- 120 grams unsalted butter, softened
- 2 tablespoons milk
- 1/2 teaspoon rosewater
- Chopped pistachios, for garnish

Instructions:

1. Preheat your oven to 180°C. Line a muffin tin with paper cupcake liners.
2. In a mixing bowl, cream together the softened butter and granulated sugar until light and fluffy.
3. Add the eggs, one at a time, beating well after each addition.
4. In a separate bowl, whisk together the flour, baking powder, salt, and ground pistachios.
5. Gradually add the dry ingredient mixture to the butter mixture, alternating with the milk. Begin and end with the dry ingredients. Mix until just combined.
6. Stir in the rosewater, ensuring it is evenly distributed throughout the batter.
7. Spoon the batter into the prepared cupcake liners, filling each about two-thirds full.
8. Bake in the preheated oven for 18-20 minutes, or until a toothpick inserted into the centre of a cupcake comes out clean.
9. Remove the cupcakes from the oven and let them cool in the muffin tin for a few minutes. Then transfer them to a wire rack to cool completely.
10. In the meantime, prepare the frosting. In a mixing bowl, beat the softened butter until creamy.
11. Gradually add the powdered sugar, milk, and rosewater to the butter, beating well after each addition. Continue beating until the frosting is smooth and fluffy.
12. Once the cupcakes are completely cooled, frost them using a piping bag or a spatula.
13. Garnish each cupcake with chopped pistachios for added texture and visual appeal.
14. Serve and enjoy the delightful Pistachio Rosewater Cupcakes!

Bananas Foster

Prep Time: 10 minutes / Cook Time: 10 minutes
Serves: 2-4

Ingredients:
- 2 ripe bananas, peeled and sliced
- 50g unsalted butter
- 60g brown sugar
- 60ml dark rum
- 60ml heavy cream
- 1 teaspoon vanilla extract
- Pinch of ground cinnamon (optional)
- Vanilla ice cream, for serving

Instructions:

1. In a large skillet or frying pan, melt the butter over medium heat.
2. Add the brown sugar to the melted butter and stir until it dissolves and forms a smooth mixture.
3. Add the sliced bananas to the skillet and gently toss them in the butter and sugar mixture to coat them evenly. Cook for 2-3 minutes, until the bananas begin to soften and caramelise slightly.
4. Carefully add the dark rum to the skillet. Be cautious as the alcohol may ignite briefly. If desired, you can use a long-handled lighter or match to flambé the mixture. Allow the flames to subside naturally.
5. Stir in the heavy cream, vanilla extract, and ground cinnamon (if using). Cook for an additional 2-3 minutes, until the sauce thickens slightly.
6. Remove the skillet from heat. The bananas foster sauce should be rich and caramel-like.
7. Serve the bananas foster immediately over a scoop or two of vanilla ice cream.
8. Optionally, you can garnish with a sprinkle of ground cinnamon or a drizzle of caramel sauce for extra flavour and presentation.
9. Enjoy the delicious combination of warm, caramelised bananas and creamy ice cream in this classic dessert!

Battenberg Cake

Prep Time: 45 minutes / Cook Time: 25-30 minutes
Serves: 8-10

Ingredients:

For the Cake:
- 175g unsalted butter, softened
- 175g caster sugar
- 3 large eggs
- 175g self-raising flour
- 1/2 teaspoon almond extract
- Pink food colouring

For the Filling and Decoration:
- 150g apricot jam
- 250g marzipan
- Icing sugar, for dusting

Instructions:

1. Preheat your air fryer to 180°C. Grease and line an 8-inch square baking pan with parchment paper.
2. In a mixing bowl, cream together the softened butter and caster sugar until light and fluffy.
3. Beat in the eggs, one at a time, ensuring each egg is well incorporated before adding the next.
4. Sift in the self-raising flour and fold it into the batter gently until just combined. Be careful not to overmix.
5. Divide the cake batter in half. In one half, mix in the almond extract. In the other half, mix in a few drops of pink food colouring until desired colour is achieved.
6. Spoon the pink batter into one side of the prepared baking pan and the almond-flavoured batter into the other side, creating a checkerboard pattern.
7. Bake in the preheated air fryer oven for 25-30 minutes, or until a toothpick inserted into the centre of the cakes comes out clean.
8. Remove the cakes from the air fryer oven and allow them to cool completely on a wire rack.
9. Once cooled, trim the edges of the cakes to ensure they are straight and even.
10. Spread a thin layer of apricot jam on one side of each cake. Press the two cakes together, jam side facing each other, to form a square shape.
11. Roll out the marzipan on a surface dusted with icing sugar into a rectangle large enough to wrap around the cake.
12. Place the jam-filled cake in the centre of the marzipan rectangle. Fold the marzipan over the cake, pressing the edges to seal.
13. Trim off any excess marzipan and lightly dust the cake with icing sugar.
14. To create the classic Battenberg design, gently score the marzipan on top of the cake, creating a diamond pattern.
15. Slice and serve the Battenberg cake, showcasing the beautiful checkerboard pattern.
16. Store any leftover cake in an airtight container at room temperature for up to 3-4 days.

Lemon Poppy Seed Cake

Prep Time: 15 minutes / Cook time: 45-50 minutes
Serves: 8-10

Ingredients:

For the cake:
- 200g all-purpose flour
- 2 teaspoons baking powder
- 1/4 teaspoon salt
- 200g unsalted butter, softened
- 200g granulated sugar
- 4 large eggs
- Zest of 2 lemons
- Juice of 1 lemon
- 2 tablespoons poppy seeds
- 120mls milk

For the glaze:
- 100g powdered sugar
- Juice of 1 lemon

Instructions:

1. Preheat your oven to 180°C. Grease and flour a 9-inch round cake pan or line it with parchment paper.
2. In a medium-sized bowl, whisk together the flour, baking powder, and salt. Set aside.
3. In a separate large mixing bowl, cream together the

softened butter and granulated sugar until light and fluffy.

4. Add the eggs, one at a time, beating well after each addition. Add the lemon zest, lemon juice, and poppy seeds, and mix until combined.
5. Gradually add the dry ingredient mixture to the butter mixture, alternating with the milk. Begin and end with the dry ingredients. Mix until just combined.
6. Pour the batter into the prepared cake pan and spread it evenly.
7. Bake in the preheated oven for 45-50 minutes, or until a toothpick inserted into the centre of the cake comes out clean.
8. Remove the cake from the oven and let it cool in the pan for about 10 minutes. Then transfer it to a wire rack to cool completely.
9. In the meantime, prepare the glaze by whisking together the powdered sugar and lemon juice until smooth.
10. Once the cake has cooled, drizzle the glaze over the top, allowing it to run down the sides of the cake.
11. Slice and serve the delicious Lemon Poppy Seed Cake.

Jam Tarts

Prep Time: 20 minutes / Cook Time: 15-20 minutes
Serves: 12

Ingredients:

For the Pastry:
- 200g all-purpose flour
- 100g unsalted butter, cold and cubed
- 50g icing sugar
- 1 large egg, beaten
- 1-2 tablespoons cold water (if needed)

For the Filling:
- Your favourite jam or fruit preServes

Instructions:

1. Preheat your air fryer to 180°C. Grease a 12-cup tart tin or line it with paper cupcake cases.
2. In a mixing bowl, combine the flour and icing sugar. Add the cold cubed butter.
3. Using your fingertips or a pastry cutter, rub the butter into the flour mixture until it resembles breadcrumbs.
4. Add the beaten egg to the mixture and gently mix until the dough starts to come together. If needed, add 1-2 tablespoons of cold water, one tablespoon at a time, until the dough forms a ball.
5. Turn the dough out onto a lightly floured surface and knead it gently until it becomes smooth.
6. Roll out the pastry to a thickness of about 3-4 mm. Use a round cookie cutter or a glass to cut out circles that fit the size of your tart tin.
7. Gently press each pastry circle into the cups of the tart tin, ensuring they cover the base and sides evenly.

8. Place a teaspoonful of your favourite jam or fruit preServes into each pastry case.
9. Optional: You can use the leftover pastry to create lattice patterns or other decorative shapes on top of the jam tarts.
10. Place the tart tin in the preheated air fryer oven and bake for 15-20 minutes, or until the pastry turns golden brown and the jam is bubbling.
11. Remove the jam tarts from the air fryer oven and allow them to cool in the tin for a few minutes. Then, transfer them to a wire rack to cool completely.
12. Serve the jam tarts at room temperature as a delightful sweet treat for tea time or any occasion.
13. Store any leftover jam tarts in an airtight container at room temperature for up to 3-4 days.

Cheese and Tomato Galettes

Prep Time: 20 minutes / Cook Time: 20-25 minutes
Serves: 4

Ingredients:

For the Galette Dough:
- 200g all-purpose flour
- 1/2 teaspoon salt
- 100g unsalted butter, cold and cubed
- 4-6 tablespoons cold water

For the Filling:
- 200g cherry tomatoes, halved
- 150g mozzarella cheese, sliced
- 2 tablespoons olive oil
- Fresh basil leaves, for garnish
- Salt and black pepper, to taste

Instructions:

1. Preheat your air fryer to 200°C. Line a baking sheet with parchment paper.
2. In a mixing bowl, combine the flour and salt. Add the cold cubed butter.
3. Using your fingertips or a pastry cutter, rub the butter into the flour mixture until it resembles coarse crumbs.
4. Gradually add cold water, one tablespoon at a time, mixing with a fork until the dough comes together. Be careful not to overwork the dough.
5. Turn the dough out onto a lightly floured surface and knead it gently until it forms a smooth ball. Wrap it in plastic wrap and refrigerate for 15-20 minutes.
6. Roll out the chilled dough into a large circle, about 1/8-inch thick. Cut out four smaller circles, approximately 6-7 inches in diameter.
7. Transfer the dough circles onto the prepared baking sheet.
8. Arrange the mozzarella slices in the centre of each dough circle, leaving a border around the edges.
9. Place the cherry tomato halves on top of the mozzarella, distributing them evenly.

10. Drizzle olive oil over the tomatoes and season with salt and black pepper to taste.
11. Gently fold the edges of the dough over the filling, creating a rustic, free-form galette shape.
12. Bake in the preheated air fryer oven for 20-25 minutes, or until the galettes are golden brown and the cheese is melted and bubbly.
13. Remove the galettes from the air fryer oven and allow them to cool slightly on the baking sheet.
14. Garnish with fresh basil leaves before serving.
15. Serve the cheese and tomato galettes warm as a delicious appetiser or light lunch option.
16. Store any leftover galettes in an airtight container in the refrigerator for up to 2-3 days. Reheat them in the air fryer oven or microwave before serving.

Pita Bread with Hummus and Roasted Red Pepper Dip

Prep Time: 15 minutes / Cook Time: 15 minutes
Serves: 4

Ingredients:

For the Pita Bread:
- 300g all-purpose flour
- 1 teaspoon instant yeast
- 1 teaspoon sugar
- 1 teaspoon salt
- 200ml warm water
- 2 tablespoons olive oil

For the Hummus:
- 400g canned chickpeas, drained and rinsed
- 3 tablespoons tahini
- 2 garlic cloves, minced
- Juice of 1 lemon
- 2 tablespoons olive oil
- Salt and black pepper, to taste
- Water (as needed for desired consistency)

For the Roasted Red Pepper Dip:
- 2 large red bell peppers
- 1 tablespoon olive oil
- 1 garlic clove, minced
- 1 tablespoon lemon juice
- Salt and black pepper, to taste

Instructions:

1. Preheat your air fryer to 220°C.
2. In a mixing bowl, combine the flour, instant yeast, sugar, and salt.
3. Gradually add warm water and olive oil to the dry ingredients. Mix until the dough comes together.
4. Transfer the dough onto a lightly floured surface and knead for about 5 minutes until it becomes smooth and elastic.
5. Divide the dough into 4 equal-sized portions and shape each portion into a ball.
6. Roll out each ball into a circular shape, about 1/4-inch

thick.
7. Place the rolled pita breads onto a baking sheet and bake in the preheated air fryer oven for 10-12 minutes, or until they puff up and turn lightly golden.
8. While the pita breads are baking, prepare the hummus. In a food processor, combine the drained chickpeas, tahini, minced garlic, lemon juice, olive oil, salt, and black pepper. Blend until smooth and creamy. If needed, add water gradually to achieve your desired consistency.
9. For the roasted red pepper dip, place the whole red bell peppers on a baking sheet and roast them in the preheated air fryer oven for 15-20 minutes, or until the skins are charred and blistered. Remove from the air fryer oven and let them cool slightly. Once cooled, remove the skin, stem, and seeds. Chop the roasted red peppers.
10. In a blender or food processor, combine the roasted red peppers, olive oil, minced garlic, lemon juice, salt, and black pepper. Blend until smooth.
11. Once the pita breads are baked and slightly cooled, slice them into wedges or halves.
12. Serve the freshly baked pita bread with a side of hummus and roasted red pepper dip.
13. Enjoy the pita bread with the flavourful dips as a delicious appetiser or part of a mezze platter.

Mini Vegetable Samosas with Tamarind Chutney

Prep Time: 30 minutes / Cook Time: 20 minutes
Serves: 4-6

Ingredients:

For the Samosa Filling:
- 2 tablespoons oil
- 1 small onion, finely chopped
- 2 cloves of garlic, minced
- 1 teaspoon ginger paste
- 1 teaspoon ground cumin
- 1 teaspoon ground coriander
- 1/2 teaspoon turmeric powder
- 1/2 teaspoon chilli powder (adjust to taste)
- 150g mixed vegetables (carrots, peas, potatoes, etc.), finely chopped
- Salt to taste
- 2 tablespoons chopped fresh coriander (cilantro) leaves

For the Samosa Wrappers:
- 10-12 sheets of filo pastry
- 2 tablespoons melted butter or oil for brushing

For the Tamarind Chutney:
- 120g tamarind pulp
- 60g jaggery or brown sugar
- 1 teaspoon ground cumin
- 1/2 teaspoon ground ginger

- 1/4 teaspoon chilli powder
- Salt to taste
- Water as needed to adjust consistency

Instructions:

1. Heat oil in a pan over medium heat. Add the chopped onion, minced garlic, and ginger paste. Sauté until the onion turns translucent.
2. Add the ground cumin, ground coriander, turmeric powder, and chilli powder. Stir well to combine and cook for a minute.
3. Add the chopped mixed vegetables to the pan and mix well. Cook for 5-7 minutes until the vegetables are tender. Season with salt to taste.
4. Remove the pan from heat and stir in the chopped fresh coriander. Set the filling aside to cool.
5. Preheat your air fryer to 180°C.
6. Lay out the filo pastry sheets and cut them into smaller rectangles, approximately 4x6 inches in size.
7. Take one rectangle of filo pastry and brush it lightly with melted butter or oil.
8. Place a spoonful of the cooled vegetable filling at one end of the rectangle.
9. Fold the filo pastry diagonally over the filling to form a triangle. Continue folding the triangle in a zigzag pattern until you reach the end of the pastry sheet.
10. Repeat the process with the remaining filo pastry sheets and vegetable filling.
11. Place the samosas on a baking sheet lined with parchment paper. Brush the tops with melted butter or oil.
12. Bake in the preheated air fryer oven for 15-20 minutes, or until the samosas are golden brown and crispy.
13. While the samosas are baking, prepare the tamarind chutney. In a small saucepan, combine the tamarind pulp, jaggery or brown sugar, ground cumin, ground ginger, chilli powder, and salt. Add water as needed to adjust the consistency. Simmer over low heat for 5-7 minutes, stirring occasionally, until the chutney thickens.
14. Remove the samosas from the air fryer oven and let them cool slightly.
15. Serve the mini vegetable samosas with the tangy tamarind chutney on the side.
16. Enjoy the crispy and flavourful samosas as a delightful appetiser or snack.

Baked Sweet Potato Fries with Chipotle Mayo Dip

Prep Time: 15 minutes / Cook Time: 25-30 minutes
Serves: 4

Ingredients:

For the Sweet Potato Fries:
- 4 medium-sized sweet potatoes
- 2 tablespoons olive oil
- 1 teaspoon paprika
- 1/2 teaspoon garlic powder
- 1/2 teaspoon salt
- 1/4 teaspoon black pepper

For the Chipotle Mayo Dip:
- 120ml mayonnaise
- 1 tablespoon lime juice
- 1-2 teaspoons chipotle sauce (adjust to taste)
- 1/4 teaspoon garlic powder
- Salt to taste

Instructions:

1. Preheat your air fryer to 200°C.
2. Wash and peel the sweet potatoes. Cut them into evenly-sized fries.
3. In a large bowl, combine the olive oil, paprika, garlic powder, salt, and black pepper. Add the sweet potato fries to the bowl and toss until they are evenly coated with the spice mixture.
4. Arrange the sweet potato fries in a single layer on a baking sheet lined with parchment paper.
5. Bake in the preheated air fryer oven for 25-30 minutes, or until the fries are crispy and golden brown. Flip the fries halfway through the cooking time for even browning.
6. While the sweet potato fries are baking, prepare the chipotle mayo dip. In a small bowl, mix together the mayonnaise, lime juice, chipotle sauce, garlic powder, and salt. Adjust the amount of chipotle sauce according to your desired level of spiciness.
7. Once the sweet potato fries are done, remove them from the air fryer oven and let them cool slightly.
8. Serve the baked sweet potato fries with the chipotle mayo dip on the side.
9. Enjoy these crispy and flavourful sweet potato fries as a delicious dessert or side dish.

Spiced Roasted Nuts

Prep Time: 5 minutes / Cook Time: 15 minutes
Serves: 6

Ingredients:

- 400g mixed nuts (such as almonds, cashews, walnuts, and pecans)
- 1 tablespoon olive oil
- 1 teaspoon paprika
- 1/2 teaspoon cayenne pepper (adjust to taste)
- 1/2 teaspoon sea salt

Instructions:

1. Preheat your air fryer to 180°C.
2. In a bowl, combine the mixed nuts, olive oil, paprika, cayenne pepper, and sea salt. Toss the nuts until they are evenly coated with the spices and seasoning.
3. Spread the seasoned nuts in a single layer on a baking sheet lined with parchment paper.
4. Roast the nuts in the preheated air fryer oven for 15 minutes, or until they are fragrant and lightly golden, stirring them once or twice during cooking to ensure even roasting.
5. Remove the nuts from the air fryer oven and let them cool completely on the baking sheet. They will continue to crisp up as they cool.
6. Once cooled, transfer the spiced roasted nuts to an airtight container for storage or serve them immediately as a delicious and flavourful snack.

Mini Beef Sliders with Caramelised Onions and Gherkins

Prep Time: 15 minutes / Cook Time: 20 minutes
Serves: 4-6

Ingredients:

For the caramelised Onions:
- 2 large onions, thinly sliced
- 2 tablespoons butter
- 1 tablespoon olive oil
- 1 tablespoon brown sugar
- Salt and pepper to taste

For the Mini Beef Patties:
- 500g ground beef
- 1/2 teaspoon garlic powder
- 1/2 teaspoon onion powder
- 1/2 teaspoon paprika
- Salt and pepper to taste
- Mini burger buns or slider rolls
- Gherkins or pickles, sliced

Instructions:

1. In a large skillet, heat the butter and olive oil over medium heat. Add the sliced onions and cook, stirring occasionally, until they become soft and golden brown, about 15-20 minutes. Stir in the brown sugar and continue to cook for an additional 5 minutes until the onions are caramelised. Season with salt and pepper to taste. Set aside.
2. In a bowl, combine the ground beef, garlic powder, onion powder, paprika, salt, and pepper. Mix well until all the ingredients are evenly incorporated.
3. Divide the beef mixture into small portions and shape them into mini patties, about the size of your slider buns.
4. Heat a skillet or grill pan over medium-high heat. Cook the mini beef patties for about 2-3 minutes per side, or until they are cooked to your desired level of doneness.
5. Assemble the sliders by placing a mini beef patty on each bun. Top with a spoonful of caramelised onions and a slice of gherkin. Secure with a toothpick if needed.
6. Serve the mini beef sliders as appetisers or a main course. They can be enjoyed hot or at room temperature.

Printed in Great Britain
by Amazon

25315511R00051